Caring School Community™

Homeside Activities

Activities
That Connect
Home and School

Grade 4

DEVELOPMENTAL STUDIES CENTER™

Acknowledgments

Homeside Activities are the product of many people—thousands of parents, teachers, and children in San Ramon, Hayward, San Francisco, Cupertino, and Salinas, California; Louisville, Kentucky; Miami and Homestead, Florida; and White Plains, New York, who piloted them.

"Homework" by Russell Hoban from *Egg Thoughts and Other Frances Songs* by Russell Hoban. Text copyright © 1964, 1972 by Russell Hoban. Selection reprinted by permission of HarperCollins Publishers.

"Moon When Deer Drop Their Horns" by Joseph Bruchac and Jonathan London © 1992 by Joseph Bruchac and Jonathan London. From *Thirteen Moons on Turtle's Back*, Philomel Books, 1992.

Developmental Studies Center
2000 Embarcadero, Suite 305
Oakland, CA 94606-5300
(800) 666-7270, fax: (510) 464-3670
www.devstu.org

ISBN-13: 978-1-57621-544-9
ISBN-10: 1-57621-544-X

Printed in the United States of America

2 3 4 5 6 7 8 9 10

A Simple Parent-Teacher Partnership for Kids

No matter who you ask, you won't get an argument about whether parents should be involved in their children's education—but you won't get many suggestions for a simple, inclusive way to make it happen, either. That's why Homeside Activities are so powerful. They provide a low-key, nonthreatening way for teachers and parents to build partnerships for kids.

These short, concrete activities in English and Spanish foster communication between teachers and parents and between parents and children. They make it easy for parents to contribute a "homeside" to their children's schoolside learning. And they make it easy for children to "schedule" personal time with a parent or other caretaking adult.

Implicit in the design of Homeside Activities is a message of respect for the diversity of children's families and communities. All activities build on the value for parents and children of talking with each other and listening to each other—in their home language. The activities recognize the social capital of the relationships children go home to when the dismissal bell rings every day. It's important for children to know that the adults guiding them at home are valued by the adults guiding them at school.

Homeside Activities are introduced once or twice a month in class, completed at home, and then incorporated into a follow-up classroom activity or discussion. Typically these 15- to 20-minute activities are reciprocal parent-child interviews or opportunities to share experiences and opinions. The activities are organized by grade level, but none of them have grade-specific references; they can also be used in mixed-grade and ungraded classrooms. The activity topics relate to academic, social, or citizenship themes that are integral to the life of almost any classroom.

For example, in a "Family Folklore" activity for fifth-graders, children learn about their own history while they collect family stories at home; then they contribute to the classroom community by sharing some of these stories in class. One classroom using this activity learned about a runaway slave who lived among the Seminoles, a courtship in which a borrowed Lincoln Continental became a neighborhood attraction, and an extended-family band that serves up the entertainment for family weddings. These seemingly small pieces of information make a big difference in how children and teachers view each other in the classroom.

BENEFITS OF HOMESIDE ACTIVITIES

	FOR STUDENTS	FOR TEACHERS	FOR PARENTS

Academic/ Intellectual	• chance to "schedule" time with parent or other adult
	• build commitment to learning
	  - engage interest of parent
	  - see importance and relevance of learning to adult life
	• build literacy
	  - communicate clearly
	  - compare information
	  - compare points of view
	  - think abstractly
	• rehearse school learning
	• reinforce school learning
	• reinforce value of home language
		• students more invested in academics because of adult involvement
		• more ways to connect new learning for students
		  - more aware of students' experiences
		  - more aware of students' knowledge
		• opportunity to inform parents of classroom learning program
		• opportunity to encourage use of home language
			• fail-safe way to contribute to child's school learning
			• exposure to classroom learning approach
			• exposure to classroom learning topics
			• opportunity to enjoy child's thinking
			• opportunity to reinforce importance and relevance of learning
			• opportunity to reinforce value of home language

Citizenship	• chance to "schedule" time with parent or other adult
	• build commitment to values
	  - engage interest of parent
	  - see importance and relevance of values to adult life
	• build complex understanding of values
	  - compare information
	  - compare points of view
	  - think abstractly
	• reinforce school learning
		• students more conscious of values
		• students more open to examining their behavior
		• students more likely to see similarities between home and school values
			• exposure to citizenship focus of classroom
			• low-key way to explore child's values
			• opportunity to communicate personal values
			• more information for ongoing guidance of child

Classroom Community	• see parents as valued contributors to classroom
	• build interpersonal understanding
	  - of individuals
	  - of diverse families/situations
	• build shared learning orientation
		• more understanding and empathy
		  - for individual students
		  - for parents' hopes and concerns
		  - for diverse circumstances of students
		• more comfort inviting parents into community
		• reinforce shared learning orientation
			• more knowledge of child's classroom
			• more comfort with child's classroom
			• more comfort with child's teacher
			• opportunity to contribute to the life of the classroom
			• low-risk forum for communicating with teacher

Perhaps as important as the activity-specific information generated by Homeside Activities are the open-ended comments to teachers that parents are encouraged to write. Sometimes the remarks let the teacher in on a child's concerns, for example, about teasing or a bully; sometimes they are simply observations, such as, "Carlos loves science this year"; and sometimes they comment on the value of the activity, as in the following:

> **"Allison liked this one. It got us both thinking and she shared more of the day's activities with me."**

> **"Tyrone says he likes doing these activities because 'your parents can help you' and because it makes you 'think about things.' I think the time spent is very special for him because we always seem to learn something about each other."**

> **"It was a good way to have a conversation with my son. I am grateful to you for the idea."**

Of course some parents might be unable or unwilling to do the activities, in which case it may be possible to find a grandparent, older sibling, neighbor, or staff member who can be a child's regular Homeside partner. For most parents, however, as uncertain as they may be about how to help their children in school, more involvement is welcome when it is introduced through specific activities within their experience and competence. Homeside Activities provide such a structure.

The particular strengths of Homeside Activities fall into three areas: academic and intellectual, citizenship, and classroom community. The chart on page 2 shows how children, teachers, and parents can all benefit in each of these areas.

Academic and Intellectual Benefits

Homeside Activities contribute to children's academic and intellectual growth in a variety of ways—most directly by providing a motivating context for children to make connections between home and school learning. Children practice critical thinking and communication skills in every activity.

Motivates Children. Children can be expected to have a stronger investment in school and academic work if it is an investment made by their parents as well. When children have a Homeside Activity to complete, they can, in effect, schedule a parent's attention and involvement.

Includes All Parents. Because the activities engage parents around universal experiences—of growing up, of having opinions, of having adult perspectives on things children are learning—the activities are inclusive and no parent need feel intimidated or incapable of contributing.

"It was a good way to have a conversation with my son."

Children

practice critical

thinking and

communication

skills in every

activity

Values Home Languages. For families whose home language is not English, the activities send the message that the school values communication in the home language. For Spanish-speakers this message is explicit since the activities are available in Spanish. For those with home languages other than Spanish or English, students will have gone over the activities in class and will be prepared to serve as "activity directors" at home.

Promotes Literacy and Thinking Skills. In doing these activities children practice literacy and thinking skills of talking, listening, synthesizing information to report to parents or back to the classroom, and comparing and evaluating information and points of view—skills that are core competencies for academic and life success.

Educates Parents about a "Thinking" Curriculum. Many parents were educated at a time when memorization and rote learning were the primary goals of schooling. Homeside Activities can introduce these parents to a "thinking" curriculum that asks open-ended questions and encourages problem solving and divergent thinking. Rather than limiting parents' role to one of monitoring homework completion, for example, Homeside Activities invite parents to participate in their children's learning experiences and allow them to enjoy their children's ideas and thought processes.

Makes Children's Past Experiences and Prior Knowledge More Accessible to the Teacher. Homeside Activities bring new areas of children's experience into the classroom, broadening the possible connections teachers can help children make when they are constructing new knowledge. When teachers and children have widely different background experiences, this can be especially important.

Citizenship Benefits

Many Homeside Activities involve children and parents in discussions of ethical behavior and principled choices about how to treat oneself and others. The activities provide parents and children with a comfortable way to exchange ideas about important values in their family.

Deepens Children's Ethical Commitment. When ethical concerns such as ways we treat a friend or how we identify "heroes" are raised at school and reinforced at home, children see their parents and teachers as partners for their ethical development. Children respond positively when the most important adults in their lives demonstrate congruent investment in their growth as kind and principled human beings.

Strengthens Children's Development as Decision Makers. The time children spend thinking about and discussing citizenship goals and ethical concerns helps them build complex understanding of these issues and prepares them to become autonomous, ethical decision makers. Homeside Activities provide a way for children to anticipate ethical choices and rehearse future behaviors.

Enhances Parental Guidance. When parents and children can exchange ideas about citizenship goals and ethical concerns in the context of Homeside Activities, rather than in response to an immediate problem, the discussion can be less loaded for both. In such a context, children may be more likely to let parents into their sometimes mysterious world, and parents may welcome a conversational approach for transmitting their values.

Classroom Community Benefits

Homeside Activities structure a way to build children's and parents' personal connections to the classroom—to create a shared feeling of community.

Invites Parents into the Community. Homeside Activities are invitations to parents to learn more about the life of their children's classroom. They are also a way for parents to become comfortable communicating with their children's teacher.

Encourages Parents to Contribute Directly to the Life of the Classroom. Information that parents contribute to the classroom through Homeside Activities deepens students' understanding of each other, provides teachers with insights into children's diverse family situations, and models the school's respect for the home cultures and family experiences of all students. At the same time, Homeside Activities do not require parents who are too busy, too tired, or too embarrassed to be anyplace other than at home with their child when making their contributions.

Reinforces a Learning Orientation. A classroom community is defined by the shared goals of its members. Homeside Activities, by virtue of their content and approach, make it clear to everyone involved with the classroom that its members are learning about learning, learning about ethical behavior, and learning about how to treat one another respectfully.

How These Activities Were Developed

Homeside Activities have been piloted and field-tested in the hundreds of classrooms across the country that have participated in the Child Development Project (CDP), a comprehensive school change effort to help elementary schools become inclusive, caring communities and stimulating, supportive places to learn. Our research has identified several conditions that children need to reach their fullest social and academic potential:

- close and caring relationships with their peers and teachers;
- opportunities to practice and benefit from prosocial values;
- compelling, relevant curriculum; and
- close cooperation and communication between families and school.

A comfortable way to exchange ideas about important values

Homeside Activities are one of the many approaches CDP has developed to meet these conditions, and over the past decade that the Homeside Activities have been used in CDP schools, we have discovered many ways to make them easier for teachers to justify academically, easier for *all* parents to respond to, and "friendlier" for kids to bring home.

FIELD-TEST FEEDBACK

Feedback from teachers, parents, and students about all aspects of Homeside Activities, coupled with our own classroom and home observations, led us to strengthen and highlight many aspects of the program, especially the following:

1 Provide teachers with introductory and follow-up classroom activities that help them incorporate the Homeside Activities into their academic programs.

2 Make the academic relevance of the activities clear to parents.

3 Make no demands in the activities that might require any resources that could exclude parents from participating.

4 Streamline the amount of information provided to parents, and use simple vocabulary and syntax.

5 Make clear that the activities are voluntary and should be enjoyable.

6 Make clear that the activities are open-ended and not "tests" of children's academic performance or ability.

7 Emphasize the importance of not grading the activities or penalizing students who are unable to return them.

8 Allow at least a week for completion of the activities.

9 Represent diverse cultures in the activity poems, quotes, songs, and other references.

10 Screen all activities for cultural sensitivity.

Guidelines for Teachers

All Homeside Activities are built around parent-child conversations and usually involve students in a short drawing or writing activity. The activities for grades K–3 are addressed to adults, and adults direct the conversation; the activities for grades 4–5 are addressed to students and are student-directed. To increase both parents' and children's comfort and success in using the activities, consider the following guidelines.

Introduce the Activities Early in the Year. During back-to-school night or a similar beginning-of-the-year occasion, personally and enthusiastically inform parents about the purpose and benefits of Homeside Activities—this definitely enhances parents' responsiveness when their children begin bringing home these assignments. If you use the first Homeside Activity in your grade-level set, "Introducing Homeside Activities," it also explains the nature of these assignments. In addition to or instead of "Introducing Homeside Activities," you might send a letter to your students' parents to explain your goals for the activities (see, for example, "A Note about Homeside Activities" on page 9). And as new children enroll in your class, be sure to communicate with their parents about your Homeside Activities program.

Explain What the Activities Are and What They Are Not. Most parents appreciate these activities and enjoy the time spent with their children, but you may also meet with some resistance from parents who misunderstand them. To preclude some possible objections, it is important to present the activities in such a way that they don't appear to be a prescription for "fixing" families or for teaching parents how to communicate with their children. Be prepared to speak with parents who expect traditional homework assignments: some may need to understand that this is "real" homework, because conversation is as important to their child's development as are other assignments. Above all, emphasize that these are supposed to be enjoyable, not a burden to either the parents or the children.

Encourage Parents to Use Their Home Language. Be sure parents understand that it's perfectly fine for them to do these activities in their home language. Point out the value to their children of developing facility in their home language as well as in English.

Use Homeside Activities Often. To see that these assignments are viewed neither as a burden nor a novelty, use them frequently enough for parents and students to see them as an integral part of the classroom program (ideally, one or two times per month). When scheduling their use, keep in mind two considerations: allow families one full week to complete each activity, preferably including a weekend; also coordinate with other teachers so that a family isn't inundated by having all their children bring these activities home at the same time.

Adjust Your Own Homework Habits. Make it clear to students (as well as their parents) that these Homeside Activities do not increase their homework load, but are part of it. This may mean that you have to adjust your own homework plans so that these activities are assigned instead of, rather than in addition to, a typical assignment.

Help Students Engage Family Members. Treat Homeside Activities with the same seriousness you use for other homework, but do not penalize students when circumstances beyond their control make it impossible or counterproductive to complete an activity. If possible, help students find ways around obstacles they may encounter; when a parent is not available, for example, encourage students to enlist the participation of other older family members or other older people. You might also have students brainstorm ways to encourage their family's participation, such as thinking ahead to when might be the best time to introduce an activity—not, for example, the night before the assignment is due, or as parents are rushing to get to work or to get dinner on the table.

Review or Rehearse the Activities in Class. All the activities are accompanied by ideas for introducing them in class and reviewing what it is that students will be doing at home. Students will feel more confident doing Homeside Activities when they have had a chance to practice or review them first. For example, when the activity asks students to interview their parents, you might have them first ask you or a partner the interview questions. In this way, students will already have an idea of what to say when they begin their dialogue with their parents; also, if their parents are not proficient in English, then the children will "know" how the assignment is supposed to go and can help their parents carry it out. Also, many teachers report that previewing the activity "jump-starts" students' enthusiasm for doing it at home.

Have Fun! Again, in considering these guidelines and planning a program of Homeside Activities, remember that flexibility and fun are key to making them work. No one needs to look for the "right" answers to questions, for the "right" conversation to take place, for the "right" products to be returned to class. Instead, the purpose and benefits of Homeside Activities are broader and perhaps more ambitious: to encourage family interactions that link children's school and home lives. We hope you will enjoy these rewarding connections among school, home, students, parents, and teachers.

Homeside

Activities

link children's

school and

home lives

Dear Family Members and Family Friends,

Welcome to Homeside Activities! Your child will bring these home to do with you once or twice a month—to add a "homeside" to the "schoolside" learning we are doing in class. These 15- to 20-minute activities

- are built around conversations between you and your child,
- deal with topics and ideas related to your child's schoolwork;
- may involve your child in a short writing or drawing activity, and
- help create a partnership between school and home.

You will find that in Homeside Activities there are no "right" or "wrong" answers, no right or wrong ways to do the activities. You can take the conversation in any direction you want, and you can have as many family members participate as you'd like. Just having these conversations is what counts, because they help your child develop thinking and language skills for life. These assignments contribute to your child's academic and social learning because

- they help you stay in touch with your child's learning;
- working with you increases your child's interest in the work;
- your child gets to practice communication skills and think about important ideas; and
- your child learns from you and sees how school learning relates to "real life."

These don't take long to do, and I'll try to give you plenty of time to fit them into your schedule. Also, teachers will plan together when to use these activities. That way, if you have several children at school, they won't all bring these home at the same time.

Thanks for taking the time to share these wonderful learning experiences with us. I hope you and your child enjoy Homeside Activities.

Your child's teacher,

Estimados padres, familiares y amigos:

¡Bienvenidos a las Actividades Familiares! Su hija o su hijo traerá estas actividades a casa una o dos veces al mes, para realizarlas junto con Uds. Esto le añadirá una dimensión hogareña a nuestro aprendizaje escolar. Cada actividad requiere de 15 a 20 minutos. En su conjunto, las actividades

- reconocen la importancia fundamental del diálogo familiar;

- tratan ideas y temas relacionados al trabajo escolar de su hija o de su hijo;

- con frecuencia incluyen una breve actividad de dibujo o de escritura y

- ayudan a crear una mejor colaboración entre la escuela y el hogar.

Encontrará que no hay respuestas "correctas" ni "incorrectas" a las Actividades Familiares, ni tampoco maneras correctas o incorrectas de llevarlas a cabo. Puede orientar el diálogo en la dirección que guste, y solicitar la participación de todos los miembros de la familia que desee. Lo importante es el simple hecho de tener estas conversaciones en el idioma que Ud. domina, ya que ésa es la mejor manera de guiar a su hija o a su hijo y de ayudarle a desarrollar su capacidad de razonar. Si su hija o su hijo aprende a comunicarse bien en el idioma del hogar, esto le ayudará a dominar con mayor facilidad el idioma de la escuela. Y el hablar bien dos idiomas le será una gran ventaja a lo largo de su vida.

Estas tareas familiares apoyan el aprendizaje académico y social , ya que:

- le ayudan a Ud. a estar al tanto de lo que su hija o su hijo está aprendiendo en la escuela;

- el trabajar con Ud. despierta el interés de su hija o de su hijo por los trabajos escolares;

- su hija o su hijo puede ejercer sus habilidades de comunicación y pensar acerca de ideas significativas;

- su hija o su hijo aprende de Ud., y puede darse cuenta de cómo lo que aprende en la escuela se relaciona con la vida cotidiana.

Las actividades no le llevarán demasiado tiempo, y trataré de darles un buen plazo en el cual las podrán cumplir. Las maestras también coordinarán el uso de las actividades entre sí, para evitar que, si usted tiene varios niños en la misma escuela, todos le traigan actividades a casa a la misma vez.

Le agradezco el que se tome el trabajo de compartir estos valiosos momentos de aprendizaje con nosotros. Espero que disfruten las Actividades Familiares.

Atentamente,

Introducing Homeside Activities

Before Sending Home the Activity

Introduce students to Homeside Activities and have a class discussion about how these activities are different from other homework assignments. Ask students to talk with a partner about what they think they will enjoy about doing Homeside Activities with a parent or adult friend, and what might be hard about doing Homeside Activities.

Have students design covers for Homeside Activity folders on manila folders or envelopes. Send the folders home with the first Homeside Activity. Have students keep completed Homeside Activities in their folders, until they bring the folders and completed activities home again with the final Homeside Activity of the year.

Follow-Up

Have students share their reactions to the first Homeside Activity. What did they enjoy about the activity? What did their parent or adult friend enjoy? What problems did students encounter? What was most interesting about the activity? Most surprising? Give students a chance to show and explain their pictures to their partners or to the class.

Introducing Homeside Activities

Dear Student,

You are in charge of this Homeside Activity, which means you are in charge of finding an adult to do it with you, finding time you both have free to do it, explaining and "directing" the activity, making sure the adult signs it, and bringing it back to class. Please find about 20 minutes that you can spend on the activity with a parent or other adult—a neighbor, grandparent, older brother or sister, or family friend. If you'd like, get a bunch of people involved!

One of the most important reasons for doing this activity is that you and the adult will learn things from each other about what you think, feel, know, and want to know. In class we can then also learn from each other, when we share what we have learned at home. Just be sure to ask the adults for permission to pass along what they say—and don't forget to thank them for contributing to our class's learning!

Tell a parent or other adult that you will be bringing home some Homeside Activities this year.

Explain that these activities ask you to talk with a parent or other adult about topics connected to your class work. Show the adult the folder you made for your Homeside Activities, and explain your design.

Talk with the adult about how the Homeside Activities will be different from other homework. Then tell each other what you might like about having these "homework" conversations.

Take notes on the back of this page.

HOMESIDE ACTIVITY

N O T E S

Ways the Homeside Activities will be different from other homework:

....

....

....

....

Some things the adult might like about your "homework" conversations:

....

....

....

....

Some things you might like about your "homework" conversations:

....

....

....

....

Comments

After you have completed
this activity, each of you
please sign your name and
the date below. If you have
any comments, please
write them in the space
provided.

....

....

....

....

Signatures   **Date**

_____   _____   _____

Please return this activity to school. Thank you.

September Start

Before Sending Home the Activity

Send this activity home after you have held a start-the-year class meeting or have reviewed with your class what this new school year will entail.

Before sending the activity home, ask the class for suggestions about making this Homeside Activity successful.

Follow-Up

Have students do partner interviews about their goals and challenges for this school year.

September Start

Dear Student,

You are in charge of this Homeside Activity, which means you are in charge of finding an adult to do it with you, finding time you both have free to do it, explaining and "directing" the activity, making sure the adult signs it, and bringing it back to class. Please find about 20 minutes that you can spend on the activity with a parent or other adult—a neighbor, grandparent, older brother or sister, or family friend. If you'd like, get a bunch of people involved!

One of the most important reasons for doing this activity is that you and the adult will learn things from each other about what you think, feel, know, and want to know. In class we can then also learn from each other, when we share what we have learned at home. Just be sure to ask the adults for permission to pass along what they say—and don't forget to thank them for contributing to our class's learning!

Tell a parent or another adult about starting off this new school year. Describe what you are looking forward to learning and what you think might be challenging.

Then interview your parent or adult to find out what was most fun and challenging for them in school when he or she was your age.

Take notes on the back of this page.

NOTES

What I look forward to learning this year, and why:

....

....

....

What I think will be challenging for me, and why:

....

....

....

What an adult found fun in school, and why:

....

....

....

What an adult found challenging in school, and why:

....

....

....

Comments

....

After you have completed this activity, each of you please sign your name and the date below. If you have any comments, please write them in the space provided.

....

....

....

....

Signatures   **Date**

_____   _____   _____

Please return this activity to school. Thank you.

A Special Offer

Before Sending Home the Activity

Have students share their thoughts and feelings about their new class with a partner. What things about the class, students, teacher, and activities are especially interesting, exciting, unfamiliar, or familiar?

Go over the Homeside Activity to make sure students understand the instructions. You might want to give an example of something you have to offer the class and something the class has to offer you.

You have the choice of asking students to share their completed activities with classmates or not. If you decide to have students share the results of the activity, be sure to let them know ahead of time that they will be asked to do this.

Before sending the activity home, ask the class for suggestions about making this Homeside Activity successful.

Follow-Up

If you decide not to have students share the results of the activity, simply ask them how the activity went and invite volunteers to share anything interesting that came out of it.

If you would like students to share their ideas with the class, have each student tell a partner about the special thing he or she can offer the class. Then have students introduce their partner to the class and tell about their partner's special offerings (if the partner is willing to have his or her ideas shared). Students may enjoy writing partner introductions, which can be illustrated and displayed on a bulletin board or bound into a class book.

A Special Offer

Dear Student,

You are in charge of this Homeside Activity, which means you are in charge of finding an adult to do it with you, finding time you both have free to do it, explaining and "directing" the activity, making sure the adult signs it, and bringing it back to class. Please find about 20 minutes that you can spend on the activity with a parent or other adult—a neighbor, grandparent, older brother or sister, or family friend. If you'd like, get a bunch of people involved!

One of the most important reasons for doing this activity is that you and the adult will learn things from each other about what you think, feel, know, and want to know. In class we can then also learn from each other, when we share what we have learned at home. Just be sure to ask the adults for permission to pass along what they say—and don't forget to thank them for contributing to our class's learning!

Tell a parent or adult friend your thoughts and feelings about your new class. Describe anything that is especially interesting about your classmates, teacher, classroom, and classroom activities.

After you have described your class, tell the adult about something special you have to offer your classmates and teacher this year. (It can be a special skill, such as drawing or knowing a lot about animals, or a personal quality, such as having a good sense of humor or being a good friend.) Tell the adult about something you think your new class can offer you.

Ask the adult to tell you about something special he or she thinks you can offer your class and something your class can offer you this year.

Write your ideas on the back of this page.

NOTES

Something I think I can offer my class:

....

....

....

Something I think my class can offer me:

....

....

....

Something the adult thinks I can offer my class:

....

....

....

Something the adult thinks my class can offer me:

....

....

....

....

Comments

After you have completed this activity, each of you please sign your name and the date below. If you have any comments, please write them in the space provided.

....

....

....

....

Signatures   **Date**

_____   _____   _____

Please return this activity to school. Thank you.

Homework Interview

Before Sending Home the Activity

Read the "Homework" poem aloud in class and discuss the general meaning of the poem. Then ask the class for suggestions about making this Homeside Activity successful.

Follow-Up

Have a class discussion of ideas for making a "very fat" task easier to do.

Homework

Homework sits on top of Sunday, squashing Sunday flat.

Homework has the smell of Monday, homework's very fat.

Heavy books and piles of paper, answers I don't know.

Sunday evening's almost finished, now I'm going to go

Do my homework in the kitchen. Maybe just a snack,

Then I'll sit right down and start as soon as I run back

For some chocolate sandwich cookies. Then I'll see what new

Show they've got on television in the living room.

Everybody's laughing there, but misery and gloom

And a full refrigerator are where I am at.

I'll just have another sandwich. Homework's very fat.

—Russell Hoban*

* From *Egg Thoughts and Other Frances Songs* by Russell Hoban. Text copyright © 1964, 1972 by Russell Hoban. Selection reprinted by permission of HarperCollins Publishers.

Homework Interview

Dear Student,

You are in charge of this Homeside Activity, which means you are in charge of finding an adult to do it with you, finding time you both have free to do it, explaining and "directing" the activity, making sure the adult signs it, and bringing it back to class. Please find about 20 minutes that you can spend on the activity with a parent or other adult—a neighbor, grandparent, older brother or sister, or family friend. If you'd like, get a bunch of people involved!

One of the most important reasons for doing this activity is that you and the adult will learn things from each other about what you think, feel, know, and want to know. In class we can then also learn from each other, when we share what we have learned at home. Just be sure to ask the adults for permission to pass along what they say—and don't forget to thank them for contributing to our class's learning!

Read the attached poem, "Homework," to a parent or other adult. Discuss what you both think the poet means when he says, "homework's very fat."

Then interview your parent or adult to find out if there's anything that feels like homework to him or her. (Is there anything the adult has to do that feels "fat" or that the adult has to do even though there are other things he or she would rather be doing?)

Ask the adult for any tips or advice on how to make such tasks easier to do. Take notes on the back of this page.

NOTES

What we think the poet means by "homework's very fat":

_____

_____

_____

_____

What feels like homework for an adult:

_____

_____

_____

_____

Some ideas on how to make "very fat" tasks easier to do:

_____

_____

_____

_____

Comments

After you have completed this activity, each of you please sign your name and the date below. If you have any comments, please write them in the space provided.

_____

_____

_____

_____

Signatures   **Date**

_____   _____

Please return this activity to school. Thank you.

A Person with a Difference

Before Sending Home the Activity

Review the activity with the class, and make sure that students understand what a "quality or characteristic you especially like" means. Have the class suggest some examples of likable qualities and characteristics. Model with a student or adult partner a conversation about a person you have gotten to know and like this year or in the past. Make it interesting!

Before sending the activity home, ask the class for suggestions about making this Homeside Activity successful.

Follow-Up

Have students tell a partner about the person who made a difference to the adult they talked with.

A Person with a Difference

Dear Student,

You are in charge of this Homeside Activity, which means you are in charge of finding an adult to do it with you, finding time you both have free to do it, explaining and "directing" the activity, making sure the adult signs it, and bringing it back to class. Please find about 20 minutes that you can spend on the activity with a parent or other adult—a neighbor, grandparent, older brother or sister, or family friend. If you'd like, get a bunch of people involved!

One of the most important reasons for doing this activity is that you and the adult will learn things from each other about what you think, feel, know, and want to know. In class we can then also learn from each other, when we share what we have learned at home. Just be sure to ask the adults for permission to pass along what they say—and don't forget to thank them for contributing to our class's learning!

Tell a parent or other adult about someone you have gotten to know and like since the beginning of school. This could be someone in your class, someone you play with, a teacher, a custodian, or some other adult at your school.

Describe your first impression of this person. Tell what you know about this person now, and describe any qualities or characteristics you especially like. Then tell how this person has made a difference to you this year.

Ask the adult to tell you about someone they remember who made a difference to them when they were in elementary school.

On the back of this page, you can take notes about what you want to tell the adult and what the adult tells you.

HOMESIDE ACTIVITY

NOTES

Someone I've gotten to know since the beginning of school: ....

My first impression of this person:

....

....

What I know about this person now/What I especially like:

....

....

How this person has made a difference to me:

....

....

Someone who made a difference to the adult, and how:

....

....

....

Comments

After you have completed this activity, each of you please sign your name and the date below. If you have any comments, please write them in the space provided.

....

....

....

....

Signatures   **Date**

_____   _____   _____

Please return this activity to school. Thank you.

A PERSON WITH A DIFFERENCE

When I Grow Up

Before Sending Home the Activity

Give students a chance to talk with a partner about what they would like to be when they grow up. Then, as a class, ask the students to share some of their ideas. Model the activity by telling students what you wanted to be when you grew up, if and why this changed, and what your strengths and shortcomings were for meeting that goal.

Help students see that it is desirable to work at something that you enjoy and which gives you satisfaction. It might also be helpful to bring in guest speakers to talk about their professions and how they chose them.

Before sending the activity home, ask the class for suggestions about making this Homeside Activity successful.

Follow-Up

Have students share their conversations with the class. If students are interested, plan some more "Career Day" activities to enhance their understanding of the working world.

When I Grow Up

Dear Student,

You are in charge of this Homeside Activity, which means you are in charge of finding an adult to do it with you, finding time you both have free to do it, explaining and "directing" the activity, making sure the adult signs it, and bringing it back to class. Please find about 20 minutes that you can spend on the activity with a parent or other adult—a neighbor, grandparent, older brother or sister, or family friend. If you'd like, get a bunch of people involved!

One of the most important reasons for doing this activity is that you and the adult will learn things from each other about what you think, feel, know, and want to know. In class we can then also learn from each other, when we share what we have learned at home. Just be sure to ask the adults for permission to pass along what they say—and don't forget to thank them for contributing to our class's learning!

When you were four or five years old, what did you want to be when you grew up? Tell a parent or adult friend about this, and then tell what you now want to be when you grow up. Talk about why your goals have changed or remained the same.

Ask the adult to help you identify some strengths you have that will help you achieve your goal. Ask the adult to help you identify some things you will have to learn to achieve your goal.

Then ask the adult to share some of his or her memories of what he or she wanted to be as a grown-up. Did this change? What helped or didn't help the adult reach that goal?

Record the ideas from your discussion on the back of this page.

WHAT I WANT TO BE: ....

Strengths I Have

Things I Need to Learn

Comments
....

After you have completed this activity, each of you please sign your name and the date below. If you have any comments, please write them in the space provided.

Signatures

Date

Please return this activity to school. Thank you.

Good News

Before Sending Home the Activity

This is a good activity to do when you and your students are studying current events—especially to show students that, despite all the bad news to be found in newspapers and news shows, the values upheld in their classroom communities are also evident and important in the larger world.

Before sending the activity home, ask the class for suggestions about making this Homeside Activity successful.

Follow-Up

Have a class discussion about the articles students read. Ask volunteers to describe their articles and the important values illustrated by the them; as they name these values, list them on the chalkboard.

Good News

Dear Student,

You are in charge of this Homeside Activity, which means you are in charge of finding an adult to do it with you, finding time you both have free to do it, explaining and "directing" the activity, making sure the adult signs it, and bringing it back to class. Please find about 20 minutes that you can spend on the activity with a parent or other adult—a neighbor, grandparent, older brother or sister, or family friend. If you'd like, get a bunch of people involved!

One of the most important reasons for doing this activity is that you and the adult will learn things from each other about what you think, feel, know, and want to know. In class we can then also learn from each other, when we share what we have learned at home. Just be sure to ask the adults for permission to pass along what they say—and don't forget to thank them for contributing to our class's learning!

With a parent or other adult, look through current newspapers or magazines to find some *good* news. Try to find an article that shows important values such as helping, sharing, or cooperating with others.

Read the article aloud together. Discuss what each of you like best about the article. Tell each other what you think the people in the article might have been feeling and thinking during the event described. Then name the important values shown in the article.

Take notes on the back of this page.

NOTES

What the adult likes best about the article:

....
....
....

What I like best about the article:

....
....
....

What we think the people in the article might have been thinking and feeling:

....
....
....

Important values shown in this article:

....
....
....

....

Comments
....

After you have completed this activity, each of you please sign your name and the date below. If you have any comments, please write them in the space provided.

....
....
....
....

Signatures   **Date**

_____   _____   _____

Please return this activity to school. Thank you.

Winter Feelings

Before Sending Home the Activity

Introduce the poem "Moon When Deer Drop Their Horns" by telling students that the Native Americans on whose legends this poem is based lived in the upper Midwest in Wisconsin and Illinois. During the severe winters there they would spend a great deal of time in their medicine lodges, large structures that housed many families.

Read the poem aloud to the class. Have partners or small groups reread the poem and discuss what they like or don't like about it. Then have the class discuss the following questions:

- How do you think the Winnebago people felt about winter?

- What might they look forward to about winter?

- What might they not look forward to about winter?

- How does the coming of winter make you feel?

Before sending the activity home, ask the class for suggestions about making this Homeside Activity successful.

Follow-Up

Have students talk about their parents' or the adults' feelings about winter and the reasons for these feelings. Then have the class discuss how adults' and children's feelings about winter are alike and different.

Moon When Deer Drop Their Horns

Now is the time when all the deer
must band together
in their winter lodges.
All autumn the bucks
fight with each other,
each one seeking to prove
himself stronger, each wanting
to be the chief of his people.

At one time the deer
kept their horns all year,
but when they entered
those winter lodges
the bucks continued
to fight with each other.
Earth Maker seeing
how the deer suffered
sent Na-na-bush, his helper,
to loosen the horns
from their foreheads
in this moon of late autumn.

Now, each winter,
when the deer gather,
just as we enter
our medicine lodges,
they leave their weapons
outside the door.
Their horns drop onto the earth,
white with peaceful snow.

—Joseph Bruchac and Jonathan London*

* © 1992 by Joseph Bruchac and Jonathan London. From *Thirteen Moons on Turtle's Back,* Philomel Books, 1992.

Winter Feelings

Dear Student,

You are in charge of this Homeside Activity, which means you are in charge of finding an adult to do it with you, finding time you both have free to do it, explaining and "directing" the activity, making sure the adult signs it, and bringing it back to class. Please find about 20 minutes that you can spend on the activity with a parent or other adult—a neighbor, grandparent, older brother or sister, or family friend. If you'd like, get a bunch of people involved!

One of the most important reasons for doing this activity is that you and the adult will learn things from each other about what you think, feel, know, and want to know. In class we can then also learn from each other, when we share what we have learned at home. Just be sure to ask the adults for permission to pass along what they say—and don't forget to thank them for contributing to our class's learning!

The attached poem is based on legends of the Winnebago tribe, Native Americans who long ago spent snowy winters confined to their lodges. Read the poem to a parent or other adult.

Talk about what feelings you think the poem communicates about the coming of winter. Then ask your parent or the adult to tell you how he or she feels with the coming of winter. List these feelings on the back of this page.

Then list your own feelings about the coming of winter. Tell each other the reasons for your feelings.

FEELINGS WE HAVE WITH THE COMING OF WINTER

Adult's feelings:

My feelings:

Comments

After you have completed this activity, each of you please sign your name and the date below. If you have any comments, please write them in the space provided.

Signatures

Date

Please return this activity to school. Thank you.

The View at New Year's

Before Sending Home the Activity

Keep in mind that you don't have to use this activity for the January 1 holiday—you could also use it at the Chinese New Year, the Jewish New Year, or any other culture's celebration of a similar holiday.

Have a class discussion about New Year holidays, asking students to volunteer what they know about how different cultures celebrate such a holiday. (Be prepared to offer information on cultures and celebrations they might not be familiar with.)

Before sending the activity home, ask the class for suggestions about making this Homeside Activity successful.

Follow-Up

Have a class discussion about what students learned the New Year holiday can mean to different people. Then discuss and agree on a few New Year's "resolutions" for the class, encouraging students to think about ways they want their classroom community to be or to improve in the new year.

The View at New Year's

Dear Student,

You are in charge of this Homeside Activity, which means you are in charge of finding an adult to do it with you, finding time you both have free to do it, explaining and "directing" the activity, making sure the adult signs it, and bringing it back to class. Please find about 20 minutes that you can spend on the activity with a parent or other adult—a neighbor, grandparent, older brother or sister, or family friend. If you'd like, get a bunch of people involved!

One of the most important reasons for doing this activity is that you and the adult will learn things from each other about what you think, feel, know, and want to know. In class we can then also learn from each other, when we share what we have learned at home. Just be sure to ask the adults for permission to pass along what they say—and don't forget to thank them for contributing to our class's learning!

Many cultures have holidays and traditions for marking the beginning of a new year. Use the questions on the back of this page to interview a parent or other adult about what new year celebrations mean to him or her. Take notes in the space provided.

Then talk about one or two goals that each of you has for the new year. Also note these on the back of this page.

INTERVIEW QUESTIONS

Do you celebrate the beginning of a new year? How?

....

....

What does this holiday or celebration mean to you?

....

....

How did you celebrate the holiday when you were a child?

....

....

NOTES FOR THE NEW YEAR

Some goals the adult has for the New Year:

....

....

Some goals I have for the new year:

....

....

....

Comments

After you have completed this activity, each of you please sign your name and the date below. If you have any comments, please write them in the space provided.

....

....

....

....

Signatures

Date

_____   _____   _____

Please return this activity to school. Thank you.

Across Generations

Before Sending Home the Activity

This activity is a good complement to schoolwide activities that strengthen relationships between adults and children in the community, or on its own it can be used to highlight the value of such relationships. Introduce the activity by revisiting the idea that "community" encompasses all the people we interact with both in school and at home, child and adult.

Point out that by their age, students know many people outside their families and have many relationships with adults other than their parents. Have students brainstorm some categories of adults with whom they have relationships—coaches, teachers, school nurses, secretaries, librarians, custodians, friends' parents, parents' friends, neighbors, shopkeepers, and so on.

Ask students to talk with a partner about an adult who is a friend. What do they like about the adult? What makes the adult a friend to them? Have partners talk about the benefits of having a friendship with an older person.

Before sending the activity home, ask the class for suggestions about making this Homeside Activity successful.

Follow-Up

Give students a chance to tell classmates about doing the Homeside Activity and to describe anything that was especially interesting. Use ideas generated from the activity to have a class discussion about the benefits to adults and young people of having friends of other generations. You may want to use the information to construct a Venn diagram about benefits to adults and young people of such friendships.

Two books in which friendships between younger and older people play key roles are *Taking Care of Yoki*, by Barbara Campbell, and *The Best Bad Thing*, by Yoshiko Uchida. In Spanish, we recommend *La abuelita Opalina*, by María Puncel, and *Guillermo Jorge Manuel José*, by Mem Fox. If this Homeside Activity stimulates a lot of discussion and thought, you may want to follow it up by reading one of these stories to the class.

Across Generations

Dear Student,

You are in charge of this Homeside Activity, which means you are in charge of finding an adult to do it with you, finding time you both have free to do it, explaining and "directing" the activity, making sure the adult signs it, and bringing it back to class. Please find about 20 minutes that you can spend on the activity with a parent or other adult—a neighbor, grandparent, older brother or sister, or family friend. If you'd like, get a bunch of people involved!

One of the most important reasons for doing this activity is that you and the adult will learn things from each other about what you think, feel, know, and want to know. In class we can then also learn from each other, when we share what we have learned at home. Just be sure to ask the adults for permission to pass along what they say—and don't forget to thank them for contributing to our class's learning!

Tell a parent or other adult about an adult who is your friend. Discuss the benefits to you of having an adult friend.

Ask the adult to tell you about a child with whom he or she is friendly. Ask the adult to tell you how he or she has benefited from having a young friend.

Use the back of this page to take notes about the benefits to each of you of your friendships across generations.

FRIENDS ACROSS GENERATIONS

The Benefits to Me of Having an Adult Friend:

The Benefits to the Adult of Having a Young Friend:

Comments

After you have completed this activity, each of you please sign your name and the date below. If you have any comments, please write them in the space provided.

Signatures

Date

Please return this activity to school. Thank you.

Historical Heroes

Before Sending Home the Activity

A week or so before sending the activity home, have each student choose a historical figure whom they admire from a period or civilization the class is studying. Have students write a monologue in the voice of that person. The monologues might narrate an important event or occasion in which the person participated, tell something about the kind of person he or she was, or tell about the times in which the person lived. Present a monologue you have written to help students see the possibilities of that dramatic form. Give students a chance to practice reading aloud or performing their monologues for classmates.

Before sending the activity home, ask the class for suggestions about making this Homeside Activity successful.

Follow-Up

Invite volunteers to tell about doing the activity at home and to report on the historical figures their adults admired. What did students learn about history? About the adult?

Historical Heroes

Dear Student,

You are in charge of this Homeside Activity, which means you are in charge of finding an adult to do it with you, finding time you both have free to do it, explaining and "directing" the activity, making sure the adult signs it, and bringing it back to class. Please find about 20 minutes that you can spend on the activity with a parent or other adult—a neighbor, grandparent, older brother or sister, or family friend. If you'd like, get a bunch of people involved!

One of the most important reasons for doing this activity is that you and the adult will learn things from each other about what you think, feel, know, and want to know. In class we can then also learn from each other, when we share what we have learned at home. Just be sure to ask the adults for permission to pass along what they say—and don't forget to thank them for contributing to our class's learning!

Introduce your adult to the historical figure you chose to study in class. Read the monologue you wrote in that person's voice. Explain why you admire that person and describe some of the things you learned about him or her.

Then ask the adult to tell you about a historical figure he or she admires, and why.

On the back of this page, write the name of that person and take notes about why the adult admires the person.

NOTES

The historical person the adult admires: ....

Reasons the adult admires this person:

....

....

....

....

....

....

....

....

....

....

....

....

Comments

After you have completed this activity, each of you please sign your name and the date below. If you have any comments, please write them in the space provided.

....

....

....

....

....

Signatures

Date

Please return this activity to school. Thank you.

Good Job!

Before Sending Home the Activity

Use this activity as an opportunity to review your classroom jobs. Are students doing their jobs respectfully and responsibly? Evaluate whether any new jobs or changes in current jobs are needed. Explain the Homeside Activity and have students suggest how they might use Venn diagrams to compare their favorite job and the favorite job of the adult. You might also model the activity, comparing your own favorite job at home and at school.

Before sending the activity home, ask the class for suggestions about making this Homeside Activity successful.

Follow-Up

Give students an opportunity to describe doing the activity at home and anything especially interesting they learned. Have a class or partner discussion about similarities and differences between favorite student and adult jobs.

Good Job!

Dear Student,

You are in charge of this Homeside Activity, which means you are in charge of finding an adult to do it with you, finding time you both have free to do it, explaining and "directing" the activity, making sure the adult signs it, and bringing it back to class. Please find about 20 minutes that you can spend on the activity with a parent or other adult—a neighbor, grandparent, older brother or sister, or family friend. If you'd like, get a bunch of people involved!

One of the most important reasons for doing this activity is that you and the adult will learn things from each other about what you think, feel, know, and want to know. In class we can then also learn from each other, when we share what we have learned at home. Just be sure to ask the adults for permission to pass along what they say—and don't forget to thank them for contributing to our class's learning!

Describe to a parent or adult friend some jobs that students do in your classroom. Tell the adult about the job you like best. Then ask the adult to tell you about some of the jobs he or she does at work or at home. Ask which job the adult likes best. On the back of this page, create a Venn diagram comparing each of your favorite jobs.

If you like, use some of the following questions to help you talk about your jobs. (You don't need to write down answers.)

- What are some of the jobs you do at home or at work?

- Which one is your favorite?

- Why do you like the job?

- What is hard about the job?

- What is easy?

- How is the job helpful to you?

- How is it helpful to others?

MY FAVORITE JOB   **ADULT'S FAVORITE JOB**

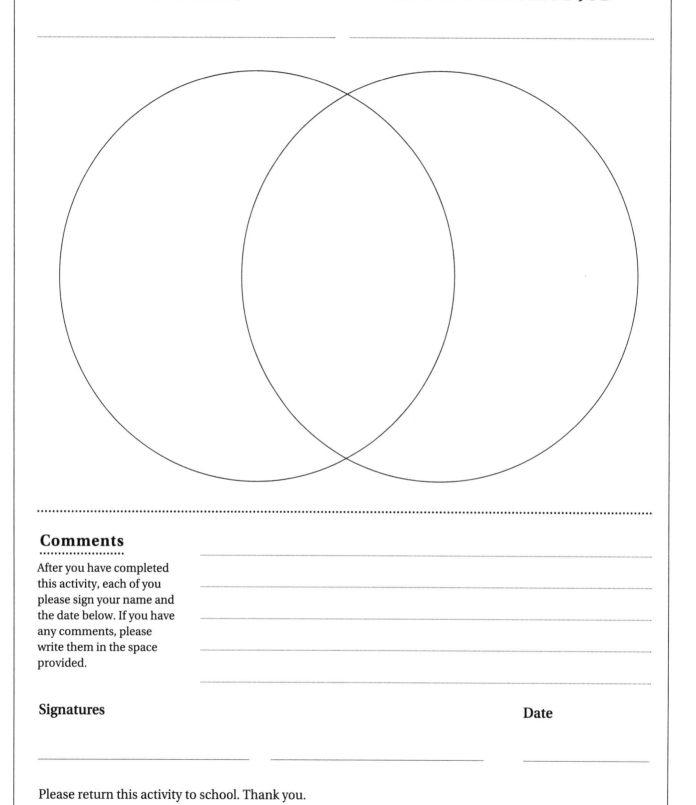

Comments

After you have completed this activity, each of you please sign your name and the date below. If you have any comments, please write them in the space provided.

Signatures   **Date**

Please return this activity to school. Thank you.

GOOD JOB!

Mirror Game

Before Sending Home the Activity

Explain the "rules" of the Mirror Game to students:

1 The game is played in pairs; one partner is the leader and one is the "mirror," and the leader and mirror may not talk to each other during the game.

2 To play the game, partners face one another; the leader moves slowly, and the partner mimics the leader's movements as though he or she were a reflection of the leader. (For example, if the leader sticks his or his right arm out to the side, the mirror "reflects" that by sticking out his or her left arm.)

3 Leader and mirror change roles and play again.

Emphasize for students that this is a cooperative game and the goal is to move together—not to "trick" their partners. Model how students will have to adjust their movements to their partners; if the mirror cannot follow, for example, the leader might slow down. At first, students may want to move just one part or their body (head, arms, etc.) or move very simply, but as they become more skilled at communicating with their partner, they can do more complicated movements. The game can also be played to music.

After playing, have students talk about how they felt playing the game, what was hard, what was enjoyable, any accommodations they had to make to one another, etc. Then explain that you want them to play the game at home with a parent or other adult.

Follow-up

Invite students to share how the activity went at home. Use the Homeside Activity as the basis for a discussion about different ways people communicate—for example, by speech, facial expressions, body language, even intuition. Discuss similarities and differences between (or benefits and burdens of) speaking and other forms of communication.

Mirror Game

Dear Student,
....

You are in charge of this Homeside Activity, which means you are in charge of finding an adult to do it with you, finding time you both have free to do it, explaining and "directing" the activity, making sure the adult signs it, and bringing it back to class. Please find about 20 minutes that you can spend on the activity with a parent or other adult—a neighbor, grandparent, older brother or sister, or family friend. If you'd like, get a bunch of people involved!

One of the most important reasons for doing this activity is that you and the adult will learn things from each other about what you think, feel, know, and want to know. In class we can then also learn from each other, when we share what we have learned at home. Just be sure to ask the adults for permission to pass along what they say—and don't forget to thank them for contributing to our class's learning!

Homeside Activities usually ask you to communicate with a parent or other adult by talking—but for this Homeside Activity, you and the adult will first communicate *without* talking! Teach a parent or other adult the Mirror Game you learned in class and then play the game together, taking turns being the leader and the follower. Talk about playing the game:.

• How did each of you feel about it?

• What are some ways you communicated while playing the game?

• What adjustments did you make for each other?

On the back of this page, fill in the Venn diagram comparing talking with playing the Mirror Game.

TALKING   **PLAYING THE MIRROR GAME**

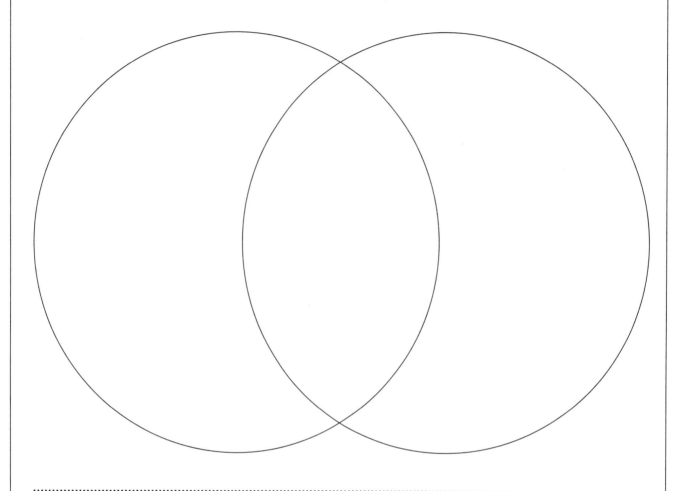

Comments

After you have completed
this activity, each of you
please sign your name and
the date below. If you have
any comments, please
write them in the space
provided.

Signatures   **Date**

Please return this activity to school. Thank you.

A Photo Story

Before Sending Home the Activity

Give students some experience telling and then writing the story of a photograph. For example, have students work in pairs, and give each partner a different picture to write about. First have them tell each other the story of their photos, then have them write their stories and read them to each other. (You might give students experience both with pictures that tell a factual story and pictures that leave room for their imagination.)

Before sending the activity home, ask the class for suggestions about making this Homeside Activity successful.

Follow-Up

Have partners read each other their stories of their family photos, and then have students draw the "photo" they imagine their partner described.

A Photo Story

Dear Student,

You are in charge of this Homeside Activity, which means you are in charge of finding an adult to do it with you, finding time you both have free to do it, explaining and "directing" the activity, making sure the adult signs it, and bringing it back to class. Please find about 20 minutes that you can spend on the activity with a parent or other adult—a neighbor, grandparent, older brother or sister, or family friend. If you'd like, get a bunch of people involved!

One of the most important reasons for doing this activity is that you and the adult will learn things from each other about what you think, feel, know, and want to know. In class we can then also learn from each other, when we share what we have learned at home. Just be sure to ask the adults for permission to pass along what they say—and don't forget to thank them for contributing to our class's learning!

Tell your parent or adult friend about a story you wrote in class that started from a photograph.

Then look at some family photographs together and decide on one to write about. Talk about what the photograph shows and what would be interesting to tell other people about it.

Then write a first draft of the story of the photograph (use a different sheet of paper). Read your first draft to the adult and decide whether there is anything you want to change before you read it to the class.

Write your final draft on the back of this page. Give your story a title, too!

PHOTO STORY

....

(title)

_____

_____

_____

_____

_____

_____

_____

_____

_____

_____

_____

_____

_____

Comments
....

After you have completed
this activity, each of you
please sign your name and
the date below. If you have
any comments, please
write them in the space
provided.

Signatures

Date

_____ _____ _____

Please return this activity to school. Thank you.

....

Neighborhood Map

Before Sending Home the Activity

Have a class discussion about neighborhoods. Ask students for their own definitions of what a neighborhood is. Explain that a neighborhood often has no specific boundaries, but is defined by how a person feels about the places and people who live around him or her. Two people in the same family might include different places in their descriptions of their neighborhood. Help students think about their neighborhoods by posing such questions as the following:

- What places are near your home?
- Which public buildings do you go to in your neighborhood (for example, stores, restaurants, libraries, schools, churches)?
- Which public places do you go to (for example, parks, playgrounds, empty lots)?
- Are there places you can or cannot go by yourself?
- Who do you know?
- Whose homes do you visit? What do you do there?

Have students draw maps of their neighborhoods, including all the people, places, and things that are important to him or her. Emphasize personal rather than objective accuracy (one child doing this activity gave special attention to the mud puddle in his front yard).

Then have the class brainstorm a list of interview questions they could ask parents or other adults about the adults' childhood neighborhoods. Encourage students to write on their Homeside Activity sheet any of the questions they want to use at home.

Before sending the activity home, ask the class for suggestions about making this Homeside Activity successful.

Follow-Up

Have partners interview each other about their neighborhood maps. Have them also compare the information they found out from their interviews at home.

Neighborhood Map

Dear Student,
....

You are in charge of this Homeside Activity, which means you are in charge of finding an adult to do it with you, finding time you both have free to do it, explaining and "directing" the activity, making sure the adult signs it, and bringing it back to class. Please find about 20 minutes that you can spend on the activity with a parent or other adult—a neighbor, grandparent, older brother or sister, or family friend. If you'd like, get a bunch of people involved!

One of the most important reasons for doing this activity is that you and the adult will learn things from each other about what you think, feel, know, and want to know. In class we can then also learn from each other, when we share what we have learned at home. Just be sure to ask the adults for permission to pass along what they say—and don't forget to thank them for contributing to our class's learning!

Tell a parent or other adult about the map you made of your neighborhood. Explain why you included the people, places, and things that you did.

Tell about your favorite and least favorite places in the neighborhood. Tell about the people you know and what you do with them.

Then ask the adult to tell you about the neighborhood he or she lived in when he or she was your age. Make notes about the adult's childhood neighborhood on the back of this page.

NOTES ABOUT THE ADULT'S CHILDHOOD NEIGHBORHOOD:

....

....

....

....

....

....

....

....

....

....

....

....

....

....

....

Comments

After you have completed this activity, each of you please sign your name and the date below. If you have any comments, please write them in the space provided.

Signatures   **Date**

_____   _____   _____

Please return this activity to school. Thank you.

Good-bye to the School Year

Before Sending Home the Activity

Have students brainstorm all the events, incidents, activities, and situations from this school year they can remember. List them for all to see. Be sure to throw in a few funny or special memories of your own. Ask students to write a farewell letter to the school year using the list and their own hearts and minds as inspiration. What was noteworthy about the year? What will students especially miss about the special mix of people who comprise the class? About their studies this year? About you (their teacher)? What won't they miss? What are students looking forward to next year? Have students share their first drafts with a partner for feedback, and then have them write final copies on the back of the Homeside Activity page. Students may enjoy illustrating their final versions with cartoons or more serious drawings.

Before sending the activity home, ask the class for suggestions about making this Homeside Activity successful.

Follow-Up

Have a discussion in which students have a chance to reflect on and share their feelings about saying good-bye to the year.

Good-bye to the School Year

Dear Student,

You are in charge of this Homeside Activity, which means you are in charge of finding an adult to do it with you, finding time you both have free to do it, explaining and "directing" the activity, making sure the adult signs it, and bringing it back to class. Please find about 20 minutes that you can spend on the activity with a parent or other adult—a neighbor, grandparent, older brother or sister, or family friend. If you'd like, get a bunch of people involved!

One of the most important reasons for doing this activity is that you and the adult will learn things from each other about what you think, feel, know, and want to know. In class we can then also learn from each other, when we share what we have learned at home. Just be sure to ask the adults for permission to pass along what they say—and don't forget to thank them for contributing to our class's learning!

Read your "good-bye" letter to a parent or adult friend. Talk with the adult about the letter, your feelings about the year, and your feelings about ending the school year.

Ask the adult to write or dictate a "P.S." sentence or two for your letter, saying what he or she remembers about your school year.

DEAR SCHOOL YEAR,

_____

_____

_____

_____

_____

_____

_____

_____

_____

P.S.

_____

_____

....

Comments

After you have completed
this activity, each of you
please sign your name and
the date below. If you have
any comments, please
write them in the space
provided.

_____

_____

_____

_____

_____

Signatures   **Date**

_____   _____   _____

Please return this activity to school. Thank you.

School Year Summary

Before Sending Home the Activity

This is a good activity to do in conjunction with an "end-the-year" activity. Before sending the activity home, ask the class for suggestions about making this Homeside Activity successful.

Follow-Up

Have partners interview each other about their memories of the school year and the memories of the adults they interviewed. Encourage them to discuss any similarities and differences between their favorite memories and the adults' favorite memories. If they're the same, why might that be? If they're different, why might that be?

School Year Summary

Dear Student,

You are in charge of this Homeside Activity, which means you are in charge of finding an adult to do it with you, finding time you both have free to do it, explaining and "directing" the activity, making sure the adult signs it, and bringing it back to class. Please find about 20 minutes that you can spend on the activity with a parent or other adult—a neighbor, grandparent, older brother or sister, or family friend. If you'd like, get a bunch of people involved!

One of the most important reasons for doing this activity is that you and the adult will learn things from each other about what you think, feel, know, and want to know. In class we can then also learn from each other, when we share what we have learned at home. Just be sure to ask the adults for permission to pass along what they say—and don't forget to thank them for contributing to our class's learning!

Discuss this past school year with a parent or other adult. Review your favorite and least favorite memories of the year.

Then find out some of the things the adult remembers about your year in school. What is the adult's favorite memory?

Take notes on the back of this page.

NOTES

My favorite memories of my school year:

....

....

....

My least favorite memories of my school year:

....

....

....

Adult's favorite memories of my school year:

....

....

....

Comments

After you have completed this activity, each of you please sign your name and the date below. If you have any comments, please write them in the space provided.

....

....

....

....

Signatures   **Date**

_____   _____   _____

Please return this activity to school. Thank you.

Homeside Activities in Review

Before Sending Home the Activity

Have a class discussion about how Homeside Activities changed from the beginning to the end of the year. How did they get easier? How did they get harder? What did students do to help make the Homeside Activities successful? What did parents or adult friends do to help make the activities successful? What were some favorite Homeside Activities? Explain this final Homeside Activity, and send home students' Homeside Activity folders along with it.

Follow-Up

Invite volunteers to tell about the Homeside Activities they created. Students might also enjoy making a Homeside Handbook for future students, with suggestions for making Homeside Activities successful. Or, they might enjoy compiling a class book about Homeside Highlights that can be reproduced and taken home by students at the end of the school year so that they can share with each other the wisdom, experiences, and knowledge contributed by classmates' family members and friends. (If you reproduce actual finished Homeside Activities for this book, check with parents before sharing their contributions; an alternative would be to have students write about what they consider the Homeside Activity highlights and what they learned from them.)

Homeside Activities in Review

Dear Student,

You are in charge of this Homeside Activity, which means you are in charge of finding an adult to do it with you, finding time you both have free to do it, explaining and "directing" the activity, making sure the adult signs it, and bringing it back to class. Please find about 20 minutes that you can spend on the activity with a parent or other adult—a neighbor, grandparent, older brother or sister, or family friend. If you'd like, get a bunch of people involved!

One of the most important reasons for doing this activity is that you and the adult will learn things from each other about what you think, feel, know, and want to know. In class we can then also learn from each other, when we share what we have learned at home. Just be sure to ask the adults for permission to pass along what they say—and don't forget to thank them for contributing to our class's learning!

For this last Homeside Activity, talk with a parent or adult friend about some highlights of this year's Homeside Activities.

With the adult, look at the Homeside Activities from the entire year, and talk about the things you each did to make these activities successful.

Tell each other which Homeside Activities were your favorites. What did you like about these?

Then think of a topic or question for which you wish there were a Homeside Activity. Have a conversation about this topic.

On the back of this page, write a few sentences about the activity you created and what you and the adult discussed about it.

NOTES

My new Homeside Activity:

_____

_____

_____

_____

What we discussed about this topic:

_____

_____

_____

_____

_____

_____

_____

_____

_____

_____

Comments

After you have completed this activity, each of you please sign your name and the date below. If you have any comments, please write them in the space provided.

_____

_____

_____

_____

_____

Signatures   **Date**

_____ _____ _____

Please return this activity to school. Thank you.

Les presentamos las Actividades Familiares

Querido alumno o querida alumna,

Tú eres la persona encargada de realizar esta Actividad Familiar: te toca encontrar a una persona mayor que la pueda hacer contigo, hallar un tiempo que los dos tengan libre, llevar a cabo la actividad, obtener la firma y por último traer la actividad de vuelta a la escuela. Necesitarás hallar unos 20 minutos que puedas dedicarle a la actividad junto con uno de tus padres o con otra persona mayor: pudiera ser un vecino o una vecina, uno de tus abuelitos, tu hermano o hermana mayor, o algún amigo o amiga de la familia. Si quieres, ¡puedes reunir a todo un grupo!

Una de las razones principales por la cual realizar esta actividad es que cada uno de ustedes aprenderá mucho acerca de la otra persona: ambos aprenderán qué piensa, qué siente, qué sabe y qué quiere saber cada cual. Más tarde en la clase, seguiremos aprendiendo unos de otros al compartir lo que hemos aprendido en casa. Sólo asegúrate de pedirles permiso a las personas mayores para compartir lo que te han contado, y ¡no te olvides de agradecerles por su contribución a nuestro aprendizaje!

Cuéntale a uno de tus padres o a otra persona mayor que este año escolar traerás a casa algunas Actividades Familiares.

Explícale que para realizar estas actividades, necesitarás conversar con él o con ella sobre algunos temas relacionados con tu trabajo escolar.

Muéstrale a la persona mayor la carpeta que preparaste para tus Actividades Familiares, y habla con él o con ella de tu diseño.

Conversen de cómo las Actividades Familiares serán distintas de otras tareas.

Luego cada cual dirá qué piensa que le va a gustar de estas "tareas" de diálogo. Escribe tus apuntes en el dorso de esta hoja.

MIS APUNTES

Las formas en que las Actividades Familiares serán distintas de otras tareas:

_____

_____

_____

Lo que quizá le guste a la persona mayor de estas tareas de diálogo:

_____

_____

_____

Lo que quizá me guste a mí de estas tareas de diálogo:

_____

_____

_____

Comentarios

Después que hayan comple-
tado esta actividad, haga el
favor cada uno de firmar y
de escribir la fecha en el
lugar indicado. Si quisieran
hacer cualquier comentario,
por favor escríbanlo aquí.

_____

_____

_____

_____

Firmas   **Fecha**

_____ _____ _____

Por favor trae esta actividad devuelta a la escuela. Gracias.

Comencemos en septiembre

Querido alumno o querida alumna,

Tú eres la persona encargada de realizar esta Actividad Familiar: te toca encontrar a una persona mayor que la pueda hacer contigo, hallar un tiempo que los dos tengan libre, llevar a cabo la actividad, obtener la firma y por último traer la actividad de vuelta a la escuela. Necesitarás hallar unos 20 minutos que puedas dedicarle a la actividad junto con uno de tus padres o con otra persona mayor: pudiera ser un vecino o una vecina, uno de tus abuelitos, tu hermano o hermana mayor, o algún amigo o amiga de la familia. Si quieres, ¡puedes reunir a todo un grupo!

Una de las razones principales por la cual realizar esta actividad es que cada uno de ustedes aprenderá mucho acerca de la otra persona: ambos aprenderán qué piensa, qué siente, qué sabe y qué quiere saber cada cual. Más tarde en la clase, seguiremos aprendiendo unos de otros al compartir lo que hemos aprendido en casa. Sólo asegúrate de pedirles permiso a las personas mayores para compartir lo que te han contado, y ¡no te olvides de agradecerles por su contribución a nuestro aprendizaje!

Cuéntale a uno de tus padres o a alguna otra persona mayor cómo es el comenzar un nuevo año escolar. Cuéntale qué es lo que quieres aprender y en qué piensas que necesitarás esforzarte.

Luego entrevista a la persona mayor para descubrir qué era lo que más le gustaba de la escuela cuando tenía tu edad, y qué era lo que se le hacía difícil.

Después que hayan conversado, haz tus apuntes en el dorso de esta hoja.

MIS APUNTES

Lo que más quiero aprender este año, y por qué:

....

....

....

Lo que pienso que será un desafío para mí, y por qué:

....

....

....

Lo que la persona mayor disfrutó más en la escuela, y por qué:

....

....

....

Lo que fue un desafío para la persona mayor, y por qué:

....

....

....

Comentarios
....

Después que hayan comple-
tado esta actividad, haga el
favor cada uno de firmar y
de escribir la fecha en el
lugar indicado. Si quisieran
hacer cualquier comentario,
por favor escríbanlo aquí.

....

....

....

....

....

Firmas

Fecha

_____   _____   _____

Por favor trae esta actividad devuelta a la escuela. Gracias.

....

Un ofrecimiento especial

Querido alumno o querida alumna,

Tú eres la persona encargada de realizar esta Actividad Familiar: te toca encontrar a una persona mayor que la pueda hacer contigo, hallar un tiempo que los dos tengan libre, llevar a cabo la actividad, obtener la firma y por último traer la actividad de vuelta a la escuela. Necesitarás hallar unos 20 minutos que puedas dedicarle a la actividad junto con uno de tus padres o con otra persona mayor: pudiera ser un vecino o una vecina, uno de tus abuelitos, tu hermano o hermana mayor, o algún amigo o amiga de la familia. Si quieres, ¡puedes reunir a todo un grupo!

Una de las razones principales por la cual realizar esta actividad es que cada uno de ustedes aprenderá mucho acerca de la otra persona: ambos aprenderán qué piensa, qué siente, qué sabe y qué quiere saber cada cual. Más tarde en la clase, seguiremos aprendiendo unos de otros al compartir lo que hemos aprendido en casa. Sólo asegúrate de pedirles permiso a las personas mayores para compartir lo que te han contado, y ¡no te olvides de agradecerles por su contribución a nuestro aprendizaje!

Cuéntale a uno de tus padres o a otra persona mayor lo que piensas y sientes sobre tu nueva clase. Cuéntale cualquier cosa que te interesa de tus compañeros, de tu maestra o de tu maestro, de tu salón de clase y de tus actividades escolares.

Después que hayas descrito tu clase, cuéntale a la persona mayor algo especial que piensas que puedes ofrecerles a tus compañeros y a tu maestro o a tu maestra. (Podría ser una habilidad especial, como el saber dibujar bien o el conocer mucho acerca de los animales. También podría ser una cualidad personal, como el tener un buen sentido del humor o el saber ser un buen amigo.) Luego cuéntale a la persona mayor algo que crees que tu nueva clase te puede ofrecer a tí.

Pídele a la persona mayor que te hable de algo especial que él o que ella piensa que tú puedes ofrecerle a la clase, y de algo que piensa que la clase te puede ofrecer a tí.

Escribe las ideas que tengan en el dorso de esta hoja.

MIS APUNTES

Algo que yo pienso que le puedo ofrecer a la clase:

....

....

....

Algo que yo pienso que la clase me puede ofrecer a mí:

....

....

....

Algo que la persona mayor piensa que le puedo ofrecer a la clase:

....

....

....

Algo que la persona mayor piensa que la clase me puede ofrecer a mí:

....

....

....

Comentarios

Después que hayan comple-
tado esta actividad, haga el
favor cada uno de firmar y
de escribir la fecha en el
lugar indicado. Si quisieran
hacer cualquier comentario,
por favor escríbanlo aquí.

Firmas   **Fecha**

_____   _____   _____

Por favor trae esta actividad devuelta a la escuela. Gracias.

La tarea

La tarea está sentada encima de la tarde del domingo, aplastándola.

La tarea tiene olor a lunes, la tarea está muy gorda.

Una carga de libros y montones de papeles, respuestas que no sé acertar.

Ya está anocheciendo, y ahora voy a ir

a hacer mi tarea en la cocina. Quizá tomaré una merienda,

luego me sentaré y comenzaré—tan pronto como corra

a buscar unas cuantas galletas más. Luego veré

qué programa nuevo de televisión están viendo en la sala.

Allá todos se ríen, pero aquí estoy yo, con desánimo y tristeza

y un refrigerador lleno de comida.

Quizá me comeré otra torta. La tarea está muy gorda.

—Russell Hoban*
traducido por Rosa Zubizarreta

* From *Egg Thoughts and Other Frances Songs* by Russell Hoban. Text copyright © 1964, 1972 by Russell Hoban. Selection reprinted by permission of HarperCollins Publishers.

Entrevista sobre "La tarea"

Querido alumno o querida alumna,

Tú eres la persona encargada de realizar esta Actividad Familiar: te toca encontrar a una persona mayor que la pueda hacer contigo, hallar un tiempo que los dos tengan libre, llevar a cabo la actividad, obtener la firma y por último traer la actividad de vuelta a la escuela. Necesitarás hallar unos 20 minutos que puedas dedicarle a la actividad junto con uno de tus padres o con otra persona mayor: pudiera ser un vecino o una vecina, uno de tus abuelitos, tu hermano o hermana mayor, o algún amigo o amiga de la familia. Si quieres, ¡puedes reunir a todo un grupo!

Una de las razones principales por la cual realizar esta actividad es que cada uno de ustedes aprenderá mucho acerca de la otra persona: ambos aprenderán qué piensa, qué siente, qué sabe y qué quiere saber cada cual. Más tarde en la clase, seguiremos aprendiendo unos de otros al compartir lo que hemos aprendido en casa. Sólo asegúrate de pedirles permiso a las personas mayores para compartir lo que te han contado, y ¡no te olvides de agradecerles por su contribución a nuestro aprendizaje!

Lee el poema "La tarea" en voz alta a uno de tus padres o a alguna otra persona mayor. Conversen sobre lo que piensan que quiere decir el poeta cuando dice que "la tarea está muy gorda".

Luego entrevista a la persona mayor para descubrir si hay algo que siente como si fuera una tarea escolar. (¿Hay algo que tiene que hacer que lo siente "gordo" o pesado? ¿Hay algo con lo cual tiene que cumplir, aunque haya otras cosas que preferiría hacer?)

Pídele a la persona mayor que te dé algunos consejos sobre qué se puede hacer para que un trabajo pesado resulte más fácil. Escribe tus apuntes en el dorso de esta hoja.

ACTIVIDAD FAMILIAR

MIS APUNTES

Lo que nosotros pensamos que el poeta quiere decir cuando dice que "la tarea está muy gorda":

....

....

....

....

Algunas cosas que la persona mayor siente como si fueran tareas escolares:

....

....

....

....

Algunas ideas sobre qué hacer para que los trabajos gordos o pesados resulten más fáciles:

....

....

....

....

....

Comentarios

Después que hayan completado esta actividad, haga el favor cada uno de firmar y de escribir la fecha en el lugar indicado. Si quisieran hacer cualquier comentario, por favor escríbanlo aquí.

Firmas   **Fecha**

_____   _____   _____

Por favor trae esta actividad devuelta a la escuela. Gracias.

Una persona especial

Querido alumno o querida alumna,

Tú eres la persona encargada de realizar esta Actividad Familiar: te toca encontrar a una persona mayor que la pueda hacer contigo, hallar un tiempo que los dos tengan libre, llevar a cabo la actividad, obtener la firma y por último traer la actividad de vuelta a la escuela. Necesitarás hallar unos 20 minutos que puedas dedicarle a la actividad junto con uno de tus padres o con otra persona mayor: pudiera ser un vecino o una vecina, uno de tus abuelitos, tu hermano o hermana mayor, o algún amigo o amiga de la familia. Si quieres, ¡puedes reunir a todo un grupo!

Una de las razones principales por la cual realizar esta actividad es que cada uno de ustedes aprenderá mucho acerca de la otra persona: ambos aprenderán qué piensa, qué siente, qué sabe y qué quiere saber cada cual. Más tarde en la clase, seguiremos aprendiendo unos de otros al compartir lo que hemos aprendido en casa. Sólo asegúrate de pedirles permiso a las personas mayores para compartir lo que te han contado, y ¡no te olvides de agradecerles por su contribución a nuestro aprendizaje!

Cuéntale a uno de tus padres o a otra persona mayor de alguien a quien has conocido desde que comenzó el año escolar. Podría ser alguien en tu clase, alguien con quien juegas, una maestra o un maestro, o una persona que trabaja en la escuela.

Cuéntale a la persona mayor cuál fue tu primera impresión de esta persona. Cuéntale qué es lo que conoces ahora acerca de esta persona, y describe las características o las cualidades de él o de ella que más te gustan. Luego habla de la importancia que ha tenido esa persona para ti este año.

Pídele a la persona mayor que te cuente de alguien que recuerda y que era importante para él o para ella cuando estaba en la escuela primaria o cuando era pequeño.

En el dorso de esta hoja, escribe tus apuntes de lo que quieras contarle a la persona mayor y de lo que la persona mayor te cuente a ti.

MIS APUNTES

Una persona a quien he llegado a conocer desde que comenzó el año escolar:

....

Mi primera impresión de esta persona:

....

....

....

Lo que conozco de esta persona ahora/lo que más me gusta de él o de ella:

....

....

....

La importancia que esta persona ha tenido para mí:

....

....

....

Alguien que era importante para la persona mayor, y por qué:

....

....

....

Comentarios

Después que hayan completado esta actividad, haga el favor cada uno de firmar y de escribir la fecha en el lugar indicado. Si quisieran hacer cualquier comentario, por favor escríbanlo aquí.

Firmas   **Fecha**

_____   _____   _____

Por favor trae esta actividad devuelta a la escuela. Gracias.

UNA PERSONA ESPECIAL

Cuando sea grande

Querido alumno o querida alumna,

Tú eres la persona encargada de realizar esta Actividad Familiar: te toca encontrar a una persona mayor que la pueda hacer contigo, hallar un tiempo que los dos tengan libre, llevar a cabo la actividad, obtener la firma y por último traer la actividad de vuelta a la escuela. Necesitarás hallar unos 20 minutos que puedas dedicarle a la actividad junto con uno de tus padres o con otra persona mayor: pudiera ser un vecino o una vecina, uno de tus abuelitos, tu hermano o hermana mayor, o algún amigo o amiga de la familia. Si quieres, ¡puedes reunir a todo un grupo!

Una de las razones principales por la cual realizar esta actividad es que cada uno de ustedes aprenderá mucho acerca de la otra persona: ambos aprenderán qué piensa, qué siente, qué sabe y qué quiere saber cada cual. Más tarde en la clase, seguiremos aprendiendo unos de otros al compartir lo que hemos aprendido en casa. Sólo asegúrate de pedirles permiso a las personas mayores para compartir lo que te han contado, y ¡no te olvides de agradecerles por su contribución a nuestro aprendizaje!

Cuando tenías cuatro o cinco años, ¿qué querías ser cuando fueras grande? Cuéntaselo a uno de tus padres o a otra persona mayor. Luego cuéntale lo que ahora piensas que quieres ser cuando crezcas. Explica por qué ha cambiado tu plan o por qué sigue siendo el mismo.

Pídele a la persona mayor que te ayude a identificar algunas habilidades que tienes que te ayudarán a realizar tu plan. Luego pídele que te ayude a identificar algunas cosas que necesitarás aprender para realizar tu plan.

Pregúntale a la persona mayor de los recuerdos que tiene sobre lo que quería ser de grande cuando era menor. ¿Cambió de idea luego? ¿Qué cosas le ayudaron a realizar su meta o se lo impidieron?

En el dorso de esta hoja, anota las ideas que resulten de la conversación.

LO QUE QUIERO SER: _____

Las habilidades que tengo

....

....

....

....

....

....

....

....

....

....

Lo que necesito aprender

....

....

....

....

....

....

....

....

....

....

Comentarios

Después que hayan comple-
tado esta actividad, haga el
favor cada uno de firmar y
de escribir la fecha en el
lugar indicado. Si quisieran
hacer cualquier comentario,
por favor escríbanlo aquí.

....

....

....

....

....

Firmas   **Fecha**

_____   _____   _____

Por favor trae esta actividad devuelta a la escuela. Gracias.

¡Buenas noticias!

Querido alumno o querida alumna,

Tú eres la persona encargada de realizar esta Actividad Familiar: te toca encontrar a una persona mayor que la pueda hacer contigo, hallar un tiempo que los dos tengan libre, llevar a cabo la actividad, obtener la firma y por último traer la actividad de vuelta a la escuela. Necesitarás hallar unos 20 minutos que puedas dedicarle a la actividad junto con uno de tus padres o con otra persona mayor: pudiera ser un vecino o una vecina, uno de tus abuelitos, tu hermano o hermana mayor, o algún amigo o amiga de la familia. Si quieres, ¡puedes reunir a todo un grupo!

Una de las razones principales por la cual realizar esta actividad es que cada uno de ustedes aprenderá mucho acerca de la otra persona: ambos aprenderán qué piensa, qué siente, qué sabe y qué quiere saber cada cual. Más tarde en la clase, seguiremos aprendiendo unos de otros al compartir lo que hemos aprendido en casa. Sólo asegúrate de pedirles permiso a las personas mayores para compartir lo que te han contado, y ¡no te olvides de agradecerles por su contribución a nuestro aprendizaje!

Con un pariente u otro adulto, revisen un periódico o una revista en busca de buenas noticias. Traten de encontrar un artículo que sugiera valores importantes, como el ayudarse unos a otros, el compartir o la cooperación.

Lean el artículo juntos en voz alta. Conversen sobre lo que más le gustó del artículo a cada uno de ustedes. ¿Cómo piensan que las personas en el artículo se habrán sentido durante lo ocurrido? Luego nombren los valores importantes que se demuestran en el artículo.

Escribe tus apuntes en el dorso de esta hoja.

MIS APUNTES

Lo que más le gustó de este artículo a la persona mayor:

Lo que más me gustó de este artículo a mí:

Lo que pensamos que las personas en el artículo pensaron y sintieron:

Los valores importantes que sugiere el artículo:

Comentarios

Después que hayan completado esta actividad, haga el favor cada uno de firmar y de escribir la fecha en el lugar indicado. Si quisieran hacer cualquier comentario, por favor escríbanlo aquí.

Firmas

Fecha

Por favor trae esta actividad devuelta a la escuela. Gracias.

La luna durante la cual los ciervos pierden sus cuernos

Éste es el momento en que todos los ciervos
deben reunirse
en sus cabañas invernales.
Durante todo el otoño los machos cabríos
pelean entre sí,
cada uno intenta demostrar
que él es el más fuerte,
cada uno quiere ser
el jefe de su pueblo.

Hubo una época en que los ciervos
mantenían sus cuernos todo el año,
pero cuando entraban
a esas cabañas invernales
los machos aún
seguían peleando.
El Creador de la Tierra, al ver
el sufrimiento de los ciervos,
envió a Na-na-bush, su ayudante,
a soltarles los cuernos
de las frentes
a la luz de esta luna de a fines de otoño.

Ahora, cada invierno,
cuando los ciervos se reúnen,
en el momento en que nosotros entramos
a nuestras cabañas medicinales,
ellos dejan sus armas fuera.
Sus cuernos caen a la tierra,
cubierta de blanco con la paz de la nieve.

—Joseph Bruchac y Jonathan London*
traducido por Malena Samaniego

Los sentimientos de invierno

Querido alumno o querida alumna,

Tú eres la persona encargada de realizar esta Actividad Familiar: te toca encontrar a una persona mayor que la pueda hacer contigo, hallar un tiempo que los dos tengan libre, llevar a cabo la actividad, obtener la firma y por último traer la actividad de vuelta a la escuela. Necesitarás hallar unos 20 minutos que puedas dedicarle a la actividad junto con uno de tus padres o con otra persona mayor: pudiera ser un vecino o una vecina, uno de tus abuelitos, tu hermano o hermana mayor, o algún amigo o amiga de la familia. Si quieres, ¡puedes reunir a todo un grupo!

Una de las razones principales por la cual realizar esta actividad es que cada uno de ustedes aprenderá mucho acerca de la otra persona: ambos aprenderán qué piensa, qué siente, qué sabe y qué quiere saber cada cual. Más tarde en la clase, seguiremos aprendiendo unos de otros al compartir lo que hemos aprendido en casa. Sólo asegúrate de pedirles permiso a las personas mayores para compartir lo que te han contado, y ¡no te olvides de agradecerles por su contribución a nuestro aprendizaje!

El poema adjunto está basado en algunas de las leyendas de la tribu Winnebago, indígenas norteamericanos que mucho tiempo atrás pasaban los inviernos de nieve en sus cabañas. Lee este poema a uno de tus padres o a otra persona mayor.

Conversen acerca de los sentimientos que piensan que comunica el poema sobre de la llegada del invierno.

Pídele a la persona mayor que te cuente cómo se siente ante la llegada del invierno. Haz una lista de esos sentimientos en el dorso de esta hoja.

Haz una lista de tus propios sentimientos ante la llegada del invierno. Hablen de las razones que tiene cada cual por sus sentimientos.

LOS SENTIMIENTOS QUE TENEMOS ANTE LA LLEGADA DEL INVIERNO

Los sentimientos de la persona mayor:

Mis sentimientos:

Comentarios

Después que hayan comple-
tado esta actividad, haga el
favor cada uno de firmar y
de escribir la fecha en el
lugar indicado. Si quisieran
hacer cualquier comentario,
por favor escríbanlo aquí.

Firmas

Fecha

Por favor trae esta actividad devuelta a la escuela. Gracias.

El panorama de un año nuevo

Querido alumno o querida alumna,

Tú eres la persona encargada de realizar esta Actividad Familiar: te toca encontrar a una persona mayor que la pueda hacer contigo, hallar un tiempo que los dos tengan libre, llevar a cabo la actividad, obtener la firma y por último traer la actividad de vuelta a la escuela. Necesitarás hallar unos 20 minutos que puedas dedicarle a la actividad junto con uno de tus padres o con otra persona mayor: pudiera ser un vecino o una vecina, uno de tus abuelitos, tu hermano o hermana mayor, o algún amigo o amiga de la familia. Si quieres, ¡puedes reunir a todo un grupo!

Una de las razones principales por la cual realizar esta actividad es que cada uno de ustedes aprenderá mucho acerca de la otra persona: ambos aprenderán qué piensa, qué siente, qué sabe y qué quiere saber cada cual. Más tarde en la clase, seguiremos aprendiendo unos de otros al compartir lo que hemos aprendido en casa. Sólo asegúrate de pedirles permiso a las personas mayores para compartir lo que te han contado, y ¡no te olvides de agradecerles por su contribución a nuestro aprendizaje!

Muchas culturas tienen fiestas y tradiciones especiales para celebrar el comienzo de un nuevo año. Utiliza las preguntas que encontrarás en el dorso de esta hoja para entrevistar a un pariente o a otra persona mayor sobre el significado que tienen para él o para ella las celebraciones del Año Nuevo. Escribe tus apuntes en el lugar indicado.

Luego conversen sobre algunas de las metas que tiene cada uno de ustedes para el Año Nuevo. Anota esta información en el lugar indicado en el dorso de esta hoja.

PREGUNTAS PARA LA ENTREVISTA

¿Celebras el comienzo del año nuevo? ¿Cómo lo celebras?

_____

_____

¿Qué significado tiene esta ocasión para ti?

_____

_____

¿Cómo celebrabas el Año Nuevo cuando eras pequeño o cuando eras pequeña?

_____

_____

MIS APUNTES PARA EL AÑO NUEVO

Algunas de las metas que tiene la persona mayor para el Año Nuevo:

_____

_____

Algunas de las metas que tengo yo para el Año Nuevo:

_____

_____

_____

Comentarios

Después que hayan completado esta actividad, haga el favor cada uno de firmar y de escribir la fecha en el lugar indicado. Si quisieran hacer cualquier comentario, por favor escríbanlo aquí.

_____

_____

_____

Firmas   **Fecha**

_____   _____   _____

Por favor trae esta actividad devuelta a la escuela. Gracias.

Abarquemos generaciones

Querido alumno
o querida alumna,

Tú eres la persona encargada de realizar esta Actividad Familiar: te toca encontrar a una persona mayor que la pueda hacer contigo, hallar un tiempo que los dos tengan libre, llevar a cabo la actividad, obtener la firma y por último traer la actividad de vuelta a la escuela. Necesitarás hallar unos 20 minutos que puedas dedicarle a la actividad junto con uno de tus padres o con otra persona mayor: pudiera ser un vecino o una vecina, uno de tus abuelitos, tu hermano o hermana mayor, o algún amigo o amiga de la familia. Si quieres, ¡puedes reunir a todo un grupo!

Una de las razones principales por la cual realizar esta actividad es que cada uno de ustedes aprenderá mucho acerca de la otra persona: ambos aprenderán qué piensa, qué siente, qué sabe y qué quiere saber cada cual. Más tarde en la clase, seguiremos aprendiendo unos de otros al compartir lo que hemos aprendido en casa. Sólo asegúrate de pedirles permiso a las personas mayores para compartir lo que te han contado, y ¡no te olvides de agradecerles por su contribución a nuestro aprendizaje!

Cuéntale a uno de tus padres o a otra persona mayor acerca de una persona mayor que es tu amigo o tu amiga. Conversen sobre las ventajas de tener una amistad con una persona mayor.

Pídele a la persona mayor que te cuente de un niño que es amigo suyo o de una niña que es amiga suya, y de qué manera el tener una amistad con una persona joven le ha beneficiado.

Utiliza el dorso de esta hoja para anotar tus apuntes sobre cómo las amistades entre personas de distintas generaciones les han beneficiado a cada uno de ustedes.

AMISTADES QUE ABARCAN DISTINTAS GENERACIONES

Cómo me ha beneficiado la amistad
con una persona mayor:

Cómo le ha beneficiado a la persona mayor
la amistad con una persona joven:

Comentarios

Después que hayan comple-
tado esta actividad, haga el
favor cada uno de firmar y
de escribir la fecha en el
lugar indicado. Si quisieran
hacer cualquier comentario,
por favor escríbanlo aquí.

Firmas

Fecha

Por favor trae esta actividad devuelta a la escuela. Gracias.

Héroes de la historia

Querido alumno o querida alumna,

Tú eres la persona encargada de realizar esta Actividad Familiar: te toca encontrar a una persona mayor que la pueda hacer contigo, hallar un tiempo que los dos tengan libre, llevar a cabo la actividad, obtener la firma y por último traer la actividad de vuelta a la escuela. Necesitarás hallar unos 20 minutos que puedas dedicarle a la actividad junto con uno de tus padres o con otra persona mayor: pudiera ser un vecino o una vecina, uno de tus abuelitos, tu hermano o hermana mayor, o algún amigo o amiga de la familia. Si quieres, ¡puedes reunir a todo un grupo!

Una de las razones principales por la cual realizar esta actividad es que cada uno de ustedes aprenderá mucho acerca de la otra persona: ambos aprenderán qué piensa, qué siente, qué sabe y qué quiere saber cada cual. Más tarde en la clase, seguiremos aprendiendo unos de otros al compartir lo que hemos aprendido en casa. Sólo asegúrate de pedirles permiso a las personas mayores para compartir lo que te han contado, y ¡no te olvides de agradecerles por su contribución a nuestro aprendizaje!

Presenta a la persona mayor el personaje histórico que elegiste para estudiar en clase. Lee el monólogo que escribiste en la voz de esa persona. Explica por qué admiras a esa persona y describe algunas de las cosas que aprendiste acerca de él o acerca de ella.

Luego pídele a la persona mayor que te cuente sobre una figura histórica a quien admira, y por qué.

En el dorso de esta hoja, escribe el nombre de esa persona y algunas de las razones por las cuales la persona mayor admira a ese personaje.

MIS APUNTES

El personaje histórico a quien admira la persona mayor:

....

Las razones por las cuales la persona mayor admira a ese personaje:

....

....

....

....

....

....

....

....

....

....

....

Comentarios

Después que hayan comple-
tado esta actividad, haga el
favor cada uno de firmar y
de escribir la fecha en el
lugar indicado. Si quisieran
hacer cualquier comentario,
por favor escríbanlo aquí.

Firmas   **Fecha**

_____ _____ _____

Por favor trae esta actividad devuelta a la escuela. Gracias.

¡Buen trabajo!

Querido alumno o querida alumna,

Tú eres la persona encargada de realizar esta Actividad Familiar: te toca encontrar a una persona mayor que la pueda hacer contigo, hallar un tiempo que los dos tengan libre, llevar a cabo la actividad, obtener la firma y por último traer la actividad de vuelta a la escuela. Necesitarás hallar unos 20 minutos que puedas dedicarle a la actividad junto con uno de tus padres o con otra persona mayor: pudiera ser un vecino o una vecina, uno de tus abuelitos, tu hermano o hermana mayor, o algún amigo o amiga de la familia. Si quieres, ¡puedes reunir a todo un grupo!

Una de las razones principales por la cual realizar esta actividad es que cada uno de ustedes aprenderá mucho acerca de la otra persona: ambos aprenderán qué piensa, qué siente, qué sabe y qué quiere saber cada cual. Más tarde en la clase, seguiremos aprendiendo unos de otros al compartir lo que hemos aprendido en casa. Sólo asegúrate de pedirles permiso a las personas mayores para compartir lo que te han contado, y ¡no te olvides de agradecerles por su contribución a nuestro aprendizaje!

Cuéntale a uno de tus padres o a otra persona mayor de algunos de los trabajos de la clase por los cuales se responsabilizan los alumnos. Cuéntale del trabajo que te gusta más. Luego pídele a la persona mayor que te cuente de algunos de los trabajos que realiza en su lugar de empleo o en la casa. Pregúntale cuál es su trabajo preferido. En el revés de esta hoja, elabora un diagrama de Venn que compare los trabajos favoritos de cada uno de ustedes.

Si quieres, puedes usar algunas de las siguientes preguntas como ayuda para conversar sobre los trabajos de cada cual. (No es necesario escribir las respuestas.)

- ¿Cuales son algunos de los trabajos que haces en tu empleo o en la casa?

- ¿Cual es tu trabajo preferido?

- ¿Por qué te gusta ese trabajo?

- ¿Qué es lo difícil de ese trabajo?

- ¿Qué es lo fácil?

- ¿De qué manera te beneficia a ti ese trabajo?

- ¿De qué manera beneficia a los demás?

MI TRABAJO FAVORITO	**EL TRABAJO FAVORITO DE LA PERSONA MAYOR**

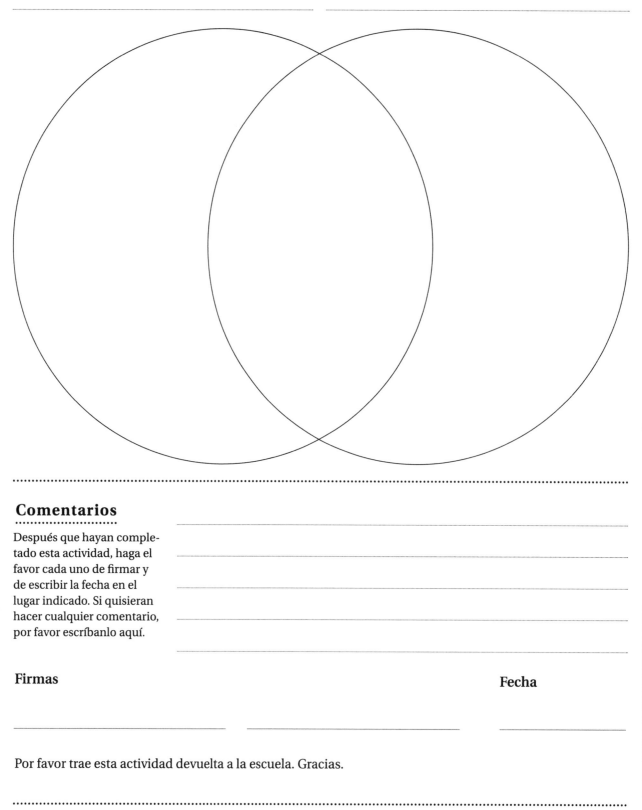

Comentarios

Después que hayan completado esta actividad, haga el favor cada uno de firmar y de escribir la fecha en el lugar indicado. Si quisieran hacer cualquier comentario, por favor escríbanlo aquí.

Firmas   **Fecha**

Por favor trae esta actividad devuelta a la escuela. Gracias.

¡BUEN TRABAJO!

El juego del espejo

Querido alumno o querida alumna,

Tú eres la persona encargada de realizar esta Actividad Familiar: te toca encontrar a una persona mayor que la pueda hacer contigo, hallar un tiempo que los dos tengan libre, llevar a cabo la actividad, obtener la firma y por último traer la actividad de vuelta a la escuela. Necesitarás hallar unos 20 minutos que puedas dedicarle a la actividad junto con uno de tus padres o con otra persona mayor: pudiera ser un vecino o una vecina, uno de tus abuelitos, tu hermano o hermana mayor, o algún amigo o amiga de la familia. Si quieres, ¡puedes reunir a todo un grupo!

Una de las razones principales por la cual realizar esta actividad es que cada uno de ustedes aprenderá mucho acerca de la otra persona: ambos aprenderán qué piensa, qué siente, qué sabe y qué quiere saber cada cual. Más tarde en la clase, seguiremos aprendiendo unos de otros al compartir lo que hemos aprendido en casa. Sólo asegúrate de pedirles permiso a las personas mayores para compartir lo que te han contado, y ¡no te olvides de agradecerles por su contribución a nuestro aprendizaje!

Usualmente, las Actividades Familiares te piden que hables con uno de tus padres o con otra persona mayor para que se comuniquen algo entre sí. Pero en esta Actividad Familiar, van a explorar cómo comunicarse sin hablar.

Primero, enséñale a uno de tus padres o a otra persona mayor el juego del espejo que aprendiste en clase. Luego jueguen el juego juntos en silencio, turnándose para ser el líder y el discípulo.

Después que hayan terminado, conversen sobre qué tal les fue con el juego. ¿Cómo se sintió cada uno de ustedes? ¿Cuáles fueron algunas de las formas en que se pudieron comunicar mientras jugaban? ¿Qué modificaciones hicieron para ayudarse el uno al otro?

Por último completa el diagrama Venn que encontrarás en el dorso de esta hoja, que compara la conversación con el juego del espejo.

LA CONVERSACIÓN   **EL JUEGO DE ESPEJO**

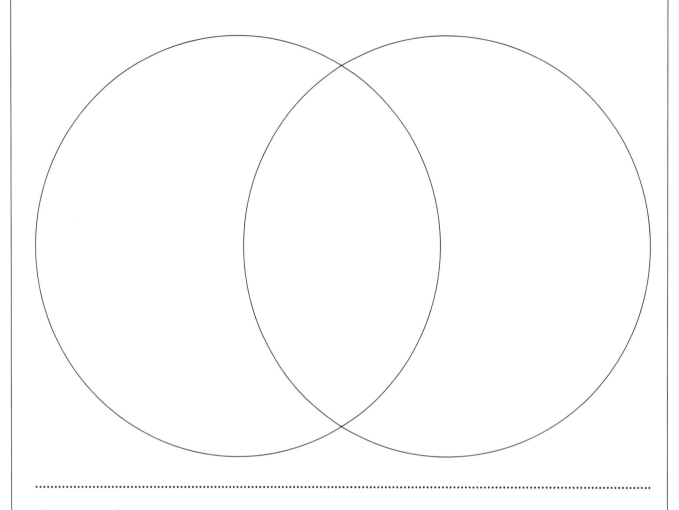

Comentarios

Después que hayan comple-
tado esta actividad, haga el
favor cada uno de firmar y
de escribir la fecha en el
lugar indicado. Si quisieran
hacer cualquier comentario,
por favor escríbanlo aquí.

Firmas   **Fecha**

Por favor trae esta actividad devuelta a la escuela. Gracias.

Una fotohistoria

Querido alumno o querida alumna,

Tú eres la persona encargada de realizar esta Actividad Familiar: te toca encontrar a una persona mayor que la pueda hacer contigo, hallar un tiempo que los dos tengan libre, llevar a cabo la actividad, obtener la firma y por último traer la actividad de vuelta a la escuela. Necesitarás hallar unos 20 minutos que puedas dedicarle a la actividad junto con uno de tus padres o con otra persona mayor: pudiera ser un vecino o una vecina, uno de tus abuelitos, tu hermano o hermana mayor, o algún amigo o amiga de la familia. Si quieres, ¡puedes reunir a todo un grupo!

Una de las razones principales por la cual realizar esta actividad es que cada uno de ustedes aprenderá mucho acerca de la otra persona: ambos aprenderán qué piensa, qué siente, qué sabe y qué quiere saber cada cual. Más tarde en la clase, seguiremos aprendiendo unos de otros al compartir lo que hemos aprendido en casa. Sólo asegúrate de pedirles permiso a las personas mayores para compartir lo que te han contado, y ¡no te olvides de agradecerles por su contribución a nuestro aprendizaje!

Cuéntale a uno de tus padres o a otra persona mayor el cuento que escribiste en la clase sobre una foto.

Luego, miren juntos algunas fotografías familiares y elijan una para escribir sobre ella. Conversen sobre la fotografía y sobre qué sería interesante contarle a otras personas de la misma.

Luego escribe un borrador del relato basado en la fotografía (escribe el borrador en otra hoja de papel). Lee el borrador a la persona mayor y decide si hay algo que quieres cambiar antes de leérselo a la clase.

Escribe la versión final en el dorso de esta hoja. ¡No te olvides de crear un título para tu relato!

MI FOTOHISTORIA

....

(título)

....

....

....

....

....

....

....

....

....

....

....

Comentarios

Después que hayan comple-
tado esta actividad, haga el
favor cada uno de firmar y
de escribir la fecha en el
lugar indicado. Si quisieran
hacer cualquier comentario,
por favor escríbanlo aquí.

Firmas   **Fecha**

_____   _____   _____

Por favor trae esta actividad devuelta a la escuela. Gracias.

Un mapa del barrio

Querido alumno o querida alumna,

Tú eres la persona encargada de realizar esta Actividad Familiar: te toca encontrar a una persona mayor que la pueda hacer contigo, hallar un tiempo que los dos tengan libre, llevar a cabo la actividad, obtener la firma y por último traer la actividad de vuelta a la escuela. Necesitarás hallar unos 20 minutos que puedas dedicarle a la actividad junto con uno de tus padres o con otra persona mayor: pudiera ser un vecino o una vecina, uno de tus abuelitos, tu hermano o hermana mayor, o algún amigo o amiga de la familia. Si quieres, ¡puedes reunir a todo un grupo!

Una de las razones principales por la cual realizar esta actividad es que cada uno de ustedes aprenderá mucho acerca de la otra persona: ambos aprenderán qué piensa, qué siente, qué sabe y qué quiere saber cada cual. Más tarde en la clase, seguiremos aprendiendo unos de otros al compartir lo que hemos aprendido en casa. Sólo asegúrate de pedirles permiso a las personas mayores para compartir lo que te han contado, y ¡no te olvides de agradecerles por su contribución a nuestro aprendizaje!

Cuéntale a uno de tus padres o a otra persona mayor acerca que elaboraste de tu barrio. Explícale por qué incluiste a las personas, a los lugares y a las cosas que seleccionaste.

Cuéntale cuál es tu lugar favorito del barrio y el lugar que menos te gusta. Cuéntele de las personas que conoces, y de lo que te gusta hacer con ellas.

Luego pídele a la persona mayor que te cuente sobre el barrio en el cual vivía cuando tenía tu edad. En el dorso de esta hoja, escribe tus apuntes sobre el barrio en el cual creció la persona mayor.

MIS APUNTES ACERCA DEL BARRIO EN EL CUAL CRECIÓ LA PERSONA MAYOR:

Comentarios

Después que hayan comple-
tado esta actividad, haga el
favor cada uno de firmar y
de escribir la fecha en el
lugar indicado. Si quisieran
hacer cualquier comentario,
por favor escríbanlo aquí.

Firmas   **Fecha**

Por favor trae esta actividad devuelta a la escuela. Gracias.

A despedirnos del año escolar

Querido alumno o querida alumna,

Tú eres la persona encargada de realizar esta Actividad Familiar: te toca encontrar a una persona mayor que la pueda hacer contigo, hallar un tiempo que los dos tengan libre, llevar a cabo la actividad, obtener la firma y por último traer la actividad de vuelta a la escuela. Necesitarás hallar unos 20 minutos que puedas dedicarle a la actividad junto con uno de tus padres o con otra persona mayor: pudiera ser un vecino o una vecina, uno de tus abuelitos, tu hermano o hermana mayor, o algún amigo o amiga de la familia. Si quieres, ¡puedes reunir a todo un grupo!

Una de las razones principales por la cual realizar esta actividad es que cada uno de ustedes aprenderá mucho acerca de la otra persona: ambos aprenderán qué piensa, qué siente, qué sabe y qué quiere saber cada cual. Más tarde en la clase, seguiremos aprendiendo unos de otros al compartir lo que hemos aprendido en casa. Sólo asegúrate de pedirles permiso a las personas mayores para compartir lo que te han contado, y ¡no te olvides de agradecerles por su contribución a nuestro aprendizaje!

Lee tu carta de despedida a uno de tus padres o a otra persona mayor. Conversa con la persona mayor acerca de la carta, de cómo te sientes con respecto a este año escolar y de cómo te sientes frente a que termina el año.

Pide a la persona mayor que escriba o que dicte una o dos oraciones de posdata ("P. D.") para añadir a la carta, dónde cuente lo que él o lo que ella recuerda de tu año escolar.

QUERIDO AÑO ESCOLAR,

_____

_____

_____

_____

_____

_____

_____

_____

_____

_____

_____

P.D.

_____

_____

_____

Comentarios

Después que hayan comple-
tado esta actividad, haga el
favor cada uno de firmar y
de escribir la fecha en el
lugar indicado. Si quisieran
hacer cualquier comentario,
por favor escríbanlo aquí.

Firmas   **Fecha**

_____   _____   _____

Por favor trae esta actividad devuelta a la escuela. Gracias.

Resumen de fin de año

Querido alumno
o querida alumna,

Tú eres la persona encargada de realizar esta Actividad Familiar: te toca encontrar a una persona mayor que la pueda hacer contigo, hallar un tiempo que los dos tengan libre, llevar a cabo la actividad, obtener la firma y por último traer la actividad de vuelta a la escuela. Necesitarás hallar unos 20 minutos que puedas dedicarle a la actividad junto con uno de tus padres o con otra persona mayor: pudiera ser un vecino o una vecina, uno de tus abuelitos, tu hermano o hermana mayor, o algún amigo o amiga de la familia. Si quieres, ¡puedes reunir a todo un grupo!

Una de las razones principales por la cual realizar esta actividad es que cada uno de ustedes aprenderá mucho acerca de la otra persona: ambos aprenderán qué piensa, qué siente, qué sabe y qué quiere saber cada cual. Más tarde en la clase, seguiremos aprendiendo unos de otros al compartir lo que hemos aprendido en casa. Sólo asegúrate de pedirles permiso a las personas mayores para compartir lo que te han contado, y ¡no te olvides de agradecerles por su contribución a nuestro aprendizaje!

Conversa con uno de tus padres o con alguna otra persona mayor sobre el año escolar que estás completando. Conversen de tus recuerdos favoritos y menos favoritos de este año.

Luego averigua cuáles son algunas de las cosas que la persona mayor recuerda de tu año escolar. ¿Cual es el recuerdo favorito de él o de ella?

Escribe tus apuntes en el dorso de esta hoja.

ACTIVIDAD FAMILIAR

MIS APUNTES

Mis recuerdos favoritos de este año escolar:

_____

_____

_____

_____

Mis recuerdos menos favoritos de este año escolar:

_____

_____

_____

_____

Los recuerdos favoritos que tiene la persona mayor sobre mi año escolar:

_____

_____

_____

_____

Comentarios

Después que hayan comple-
tado esta actividad, haga el
favor cada uno de firmar y
de escribir la fecha en el
lugar indicado. Si quisieran
hacer cualquier comentario,
por favor escríbanlo aquí.

_____

_____

_____

_____

_____

Firmas   **Fecha**

_____   _____   _____

Por favor trae esta actividad devuelta a la escuela. Gracias.

RESUMEN DE FIN DE AÑO

Repasemos las Actividades Familiares

Querido alumno o querida alumna,

Tú eres la persona encargada de realizar esta Actividad Familiar: te toca encontrar a una persona mayor que la pueda hacer contigo, hallar un tiempo que los dos tengan libre, llevar a cabo la actividad, obtener la firma y por último traer la actividad de vuelta a la escuela. Necesitarás hallar unos 20 minutos que puedas dedicarle a la actividad junto con uno de tus padres o con otra persona mayor: pudiera ser un vecino o una vecina, uno de tus abuelitos, tu hermano o hermana mayor, o algún amigo o amiga de la familia. Si quieres, ¡puedes reunir a todo un grupo!

Una de las razones principales por la cual realizar esta actividad es que cada uno de ustedes aprenderá mucho acerca de la otra persona: ambos aprenderán qué piensa, qué siente, qué sabe y qué quiere saber cada cual. Más tarde en la clase, seguiremos aprendiendo unos de otros al compartir lo que hemos aprendido en casa. Sólo asegúrate de pedirles permiso a las personas mayores para compartir lo que te han contado, y ¡no te olvides de agradecerles por su contribución a nuestro aprendizaje!

Para esta última Actividad Familiar, conversa con uno de tus padres o con otra persona mayor sobre algunos de los momentos especiales que hayan tenido este año con las Actividades Familiares.

Repasen juntos las Actividades Familiares de todo el año, y conversen acerca de qué hizo cada cuál para asegurar el éxito de las actividades.

Hablen sobre las actividades favoritas de cada uno de ustedes. ¿Qué fue lo que les gustó de esas actividades?

Luego piensa en un tema o en una pregunta que te gustaría explorar en una Actividad Familiar. Conversen sobre ese tema.

Escribe algunas oraciones en el dorso de esta hoja sobre esta nueva Actividad Familiar que acabas de crear.

MIS APUNTES

Mi nueva Actividad Familiar:

Lo que conversamos sobre este tema:

Comentarios

Después que hayan completado esta actividad, haga el favor cada uno de firmar y de escribir la fecha en el lugar indicado. Si quisieran hacer cualquier comentario, por favor escríbanlo aquí.

Firmas   **Fecha**

Por favor trae esta actividad devuelta a la escuela. Gracias.

Funding for Developmental Studies Center has been generously provided by:

The Annenberg Foundation, Inc.

The Atlantic Philanthropies (USA) Inc.

The Robert Bowne Foundation, Inc.

The Annie E. Casey Foundation

Center for Substance Abuse Prevention:
    Substance Abuse and Mental Health Services Agency,
    U.S. Department of Health and Human Services

The Danforth Foundation

The DuBarry Foundation

The Ford Foundation

William T. Grant Foundation

Evelyn and Walter Haas, Jr. Fund

Walter and Elise Haas Fund

J. David and Pamela Hakman Family Foundation

Hasbro Children's Foundation

Charles Hayden Foundation

The William Randolph Hearst Foundation

Clarence E. Heller Charitable Foundation

The William and Flora Hewlett Foundation

The James Irvine Foundation

The Robert Wood Johnson Foundation

Walter S. Johnson Foundation

Ewing Marion Kauffman Foundation

W.K. Kellogg Foundation

John S. and James L. Knight Foundation

Lilly Endowment, Inc.

The MBK Foundation

Mr. and Mrs. Sanford N. McDonnell

The John D. and Catherine T. MacArthur Foundation

A.L. Mailman Family Foundation, Inc.

Charles Stewart Mott Foundation

National Institute on Drug Abuse (NIDA),
    National Institutes of Health

National Science Foundation

Nippon Life Insurance Foundation

Karen and Christopher Payne Foundation

The Pew Charitable Trusts

The Pinkerton Foundation

The Rockefeller Foundation

Louise and Claude Rosenberg, Jr. Family Foundation

The San Francisco Foundation

Shinnyo-En Foundation

Silver Giving Foundation

The Spencer Foundation

Spunk Fund, Inc.

Stuart Foundation

The Stupski Family Foundation

The Sulzberger Foundation, Inc.

Surdna Foundation, Inc.

John Templeton Foundation

U.S. Department of Education

Wallace-Reader's Digest Funds

Wells Fargo Bank

Caring School Community™
Reorder Information

Classroom Packages

Each grade-level package contains a Class Meetings Kit (grades K–1 or 2–6), Teacher's Calendar (grades K–1 or 2–6), *Cross-Age Buddies Activity Book, Homeside Activities* (grade specific), and *Schoolwide Community-Building Activities.*

Kindergarten Classroom Package	CSCK00
Grade 1 Classroom Package	CSC100
Grade 2 Classroom Package	CSC200
Grade 3 Classroom Package	CSC300
Grade 4 Classroom Package	CSC400
Grade 5 Classroom Package	CSC500
Grade 6 Classroom Package	CSC600

Classroom Packages with Read-Aloud Values Library

Kindergarten Classroom Package with Library (10 titles)	CSCKLK
Grade 1 Classroom Package with Library (10 titles)	CSCKL1
Grade 2 Classroom Package with Library (10 titles)	CSCKL2
Grade 3 Classroom Package with Library (10 titles)	CSCKL3
Grade 4 Classroom Package with Library (10 titles)	CSCKL4
Grade 5 Classroom Package with Library (10 titles)	CSCKL5
Grade 6 Classroom Package with Library (9 titles)	CSCKL6
Complete Read-Aloud Values Library (69 titles)	CSCL00

Principal's Package   CSCP00

Each package contains Class Meetings Kits (grades K–1 and 2–6), Teacher's Calendars (grades K–1 and 2–6), *Cross-Age Buddies Activity Book, Homeside Activities* (grades K–6), *Schoolwide Community-Building Activities, Principal's Leadership Guide,* Principal's Calendar, Implementation Schedule, and Observation Forms.

Available separately

Class Meeting Lessons Package K–1 (contains Class Meeting Lessons K–1 and Teacher's Calendar)	CMLP00
Class Meeting Lessons Package 2–6 (contains Class Meeting Lessons 2–6 and Teacher's Calendar)	CMLP20
Cross-Age Buddies Activities Book	BAB000
Schoolwide Community-Building Activities	SAB000
Homeside Activities: Kindergarten	HABK00
Homeside Activities: Grade One	HAB100
Homeside Activities: Grade Two	HAB200
Homeside Activities: Grade Three	HAB300
Homeside Activities: Grade Four	HAB400
Homeside Activities: Grade Five	HAB500
Homeside Activities: Grade Six	HAB600
Principal's Leadership Guide	CSCPLG
Principal's Observation Forms	CSCPOF

Ordering Information:
To order call 800.666.7270 * fax 510.842.0348 * log on to www.devstu.org * e-mail pubs@devstu.org

Or Mail Your Order to:
Developmental Studies Center * Publications Department * 2000 Embarcadero, Suite 305 * Oakland, CA 94606

DEVELOPMENTAL STUDIES CENTER™